Twayne's United States Authors Series

Sylvia E. Bowman, *Editor*

INDIANA UNIVERSITY

Frederic Prokosch

FREDERIC PROKOSCH

by **RADCLIFFE SQUIRES**
University of Michigan

 61

Twayne Publishers, Inc.   ::   New York

To
HOWARD MUMFORD JONES

Preface

FREDERIC PROKOSCH'S first novel *The Asiatics*, published in 1935, brought him a sudden fame which diminished almost as suddenly ten years later. Looking now at the achievement of almost thirty years—twelve novels and three collections of poetry—one asks if the early admiration was ill founded; or, if the present neglect is merited; or, if certain critics are now wise, who were foolish earlier in the century. The truth is simple. Frederic Prokosch's novels are casualties of World War II. The daring spiritual search which characterized literature in the second and third decades of this century became irrelevant in 1945 to a generation that was looking primarily for a secure foothold in a corporation or in suburbia. As an accompaniment to this generation, a literature of querulous adjustments and maladjustments to society arose, along with a somewhat timid, formalistic criticism. Such criticism did not so much attack Prokosch's work as ignore it.

Outside of the perfunctory treatments in reference books, only two rather short articles have been written in America about Prokosch: Dayton Kohler's "Frederic Prokosch" (1943) and Richard C. Carpenter's "The Novels of Frederic Prokosch" (1957). Although these articles are of worth and interest, they are limited in scope. In effect, then, virtually all the criticism of Prokosch's work consists of reviews.

Reviewers have tended to ignore theme and meaning in Prokosch's novels, with the result that his emotional intensity has seemed unanchored and his characters grotesque. I suspect that the fluid beauty of Prokosch's descriptions, which, by calling attention to themselves, distract the reader from the meaning, has encouraged this unbalanced approach. Yet no critic has a right to admire beauty without working hard to find out what generates it. For there is no such thing as a style that creates itself. A style is produced by a dynamo, by some simple but powerful arrangement of forces within the artistic personality, by the flow of passion, the cerebral checks and balances.

It is a waste of breath to storm against fluctuations in literary tastes. The only successful storms are those that are going with the wind anyway. But I like to think that some calm center exists from which a criticism relatively immune to fad can emerge. If such a center exists, it does so because the human heart and mind themselves are perennial, unchanging centers. I have sought, therefore, to direct this study toward the interplay of emotion and intellect in Frederic Prokosch's work.

RADCLIFFE SQUIRES

University of Michigan
Ann Arbor

Acknowledgments

I am deeply grateful for help given me by Frederic Prokosch's sister, Mrs. Hans Kurath, as well as for suggestions from Joe Lee Davis, Donald Hall, and William Steinhoff. I wish also to thank Frederic Prokosch for a most illuminating letter.

Quotations from the poetry and novels of Frederic Prokosch are made by permission of Farrar, Straus and Cudahy, Incorporated. Quotations from Stephen Spender's story "The Dead Island" are made by permission of Stephen Spender.

Contents

Chapter

    Chronology   13

1. Introduction   17

2. The Poetry: An Analytical Note   36

3. The Wanderers   48

4. The Decadents   70

5. The Peripheries of War   87

6. The Landscape of the Soul   102

7. The Novels: A Critical Conclusion   131

    Notes and References   148

    Selected Bibliography   151

    Index   155

Chronology

1906   Frederic Prokosch, second child of Eduard Prokosch and Mathilde Dapprich Prokosch, was born May 17 in Madison, Wisconsin. An older sister, Gertrude (now Mrs. Hans Kurath), was born in 1903.

1911   Brother, Walther, born.

1913   Family moves to Austin, Texas.

1914   Attends school in Europe.

1915   Returns to America and attends school in Austin.

1919   Family moves to Chicago.

1920   Family moves to Bryn Mawr. Attends high-school.

1921   Travel and study in Europe.

1922   Enters Haverford College.

1926   Graduates from Haverford College.

1928   Master of Arts, Haverford College.

1929   Research Fellow, King's College, Cambridge.

1930   Master of Arts, King's College, Cambridge. Graduate study at Yale University. Eduard Prokosch appointed Sterling Professor at Yale.

1931-   Teaching at Yale University.
1933

1932   Doctor of Philosophy, Yale University.

1934   Research Fellow at Yale University.

1935   *The Asiatics* published. Travel abroad.

1936   Instructor of English, New York University. *The Assassins* published.

1937   *The Seven Who Fled* published as the Harper Prize novel. Guggenheim Fellowship. Gives up teaching.

1938 Death of father. *The Carnival.* Travel abroad.

1939 *Night of the Poor.*

1940 *Death at Sea.* Living in Lisbon, Portugal.

1941 *The Skies of Europe.*

1942 Returns to America to work for the Office of War Information.

1943 *The Conspirators.* Attached to the American Legation in Stockholm, Sweden. *Some Poems of Frederich Hölderlin.*

1945 *Age of Thunder.*

1946 *The Idols of the Cave.*

1946- Living abroad, primarily in Italy, with a sojourn in
1953 Hong Kong.

1947 *Love Sonnets by Louise Labé. Medea.*

1948 *Chosen Poems. Storm and Echo.*

1951 Death of mother. Fulbright Fellowship at the University of Rome.

1953 *Nine Days to Mukalla.* Brief return to America.

1954 Return to Europe.

1955 *A Tale for Midnight.*

1960 *A Ballad of Love.*

1962 *The Seven Sisters.* Living in Paris.

Frederic Prokosch

CHAPTER 1

Introduction

I *Family Background*

EDUARD PROKOSCH, the son of Wenzel and Marie Fischer Prokosch, was born May 15, 1876, in Eger, Austria, where he attended the gymnasium. After passing the state teacher's examination in Vienna, he came to the United States in 1898. In order to make a living in his adopted country, he attended the National German-American Teachers' Seminary of Milwaukee, graduating in 1900. While attending the seminary, he met Mathilde Dapprich, the daughter of Emil Dapprich, the director of the Milwaukee Seminary. They were married June 17, 1901.

Mathilde Dapprich, though of Austrian descent, was born in Baltimore, Maryland. She was a well-known pianist, who once played for the Emperor Franz Joseph.[1] Her marriage to Eduard Prokosch brought together the artistic sensibility with the scientific and scholarly.

Eduard Prokosch pursued linguistics and philology with awesome determination. In 1901 he received a master's degree from the University of Chicago and in 1905 a doctorate from Leipzig. His career as a teacher began at the University of Chicago and was continued from 1905 to 1913 at the University of Wisconsin, first as instructor, then as an assistant professor and as a professor of Germanic philology. In 1913 he moved to the University of Texas in Austin, where he stayed until 1919. In the latter year he was dismissed, along with other members of the German Department, because of the tide of anti-German feeling after World War I. At this time one becomes aware of the tough inner strength and resiliency in Eduard Prokosch. With his wife and children he returned to Chicago and learned typesetting well enough to set the type for his *Elementary Russian Grammar* (1919).

Fortunately, the anti-German sentiment in America subsided, and in 1920 Eduard Prokosch was able to secure an appointment as lecturer and later as professor at Bryn Mawr College. In 1927 he was appointed head of the German Department at New York University; and in 1930 he became Sterling Professor of Germanic Languages at Yale University. His writings, in addition to his *Russian Grammar,* include *Introduction to German* (1911 and 1924), *Teaching of German in Secondary Schools* (1915), *Sounds and History of the German Language* (1916), *College Teaching of German* (1920), *Rhythms and Personlichheit in Goethe's Faust* (1925), *Outline of German Historical Grammar* (1933) and *The Germanic Languages, their Source and Drift* (1935). He served as president of the Linguistic Society of America and of the Modern Language Association of America. As a teacher, while he held conservatively to the historical, linguistic approach to literature, he pioneered radically for the direct method in teaching languages.

In the late 1930's Eduard Prokosch developed an articular difficulty which occasionally impaired the control of his arms and legs. As a result there was official police concern as to whether he should be permitted to drive an automobile. His response to the official concern seems to have been a final example of his stubborn independence. On August 10, 1938, a few days after the police query, he purchased a new automobile. The following day he was killed when he lost control of the automobile and crashed into a large trailer truck.[2]

The three children of Eduard and Mathilde Prokosch reflect the talents of the artist and of the professional scholar. The oldest Gertrude (born 1903), became a professional teacher and student of the dance. The youngest, Walther (born 1911), became an architect, collaborating in a book on airport planning. The middle son became one of the most controversial and original novelists of the twentieth century.

II *Early Years and Influences*

Frederic Prokosch was born May 17, 1906 in Madison, Wisconsin.[3] During his early years the Prokosch family lived in a comfortable house with a pleasant garden on Edgewood

Avenue. At the age of five, though the family was not Catholic, the young boy attended kindergarten at a Catholic girls convent school. He was the only boy in attendance, but he found "the Sisters and the little girls . . . very sweet to" him. When Professor Prokosch moved to the University of Texas, Frederic was sent, in 1914, to Europe. He visited his grandfather in Eger, and he attended private schools in Munich and in Austria. Of one school, he remembers: "The boys made fun of me, called me 'der kleine Indianer,' because I was quite sunburned and besides they thought everyone from America was an Indian. One of my schoolmasters caned me almost every day, in spite of the fact that I was a very shy and quiet little boy. I don't understand it at all."[4] Despite such sorrows, he developed a love for Austria and Germany; and, when in 1915 he returned to his family in Texas, he spoke German better than he spoke English. For that matter, the Prokosch household was always bilingual.

The early experiences in Wisconsin and Texas show up from time to time in his novels, particularly in his most nearly autobiographical novel, *A Ballad of Love* (1960). Of especial importance in his formative years was a rather rickety summer cottage which the family maintained near Sauk City, Wisconsin. The sense of locale in *The Night of the Poor*—the meadowy, watery bucolic moments—derives from these summer memories of the Prairie du Sauk. It is noteworthy, too, that Wisconsin is generally associated in Prokosch's mind with "innocence" but Texas is associated either with a loss of innocence or with maturation. Whatever else came to the young boy in Texas, he must have received there his first impressions of one of his most tell-tale obsessions in the novels: the tone of grotesque incomprehension arising from an atmosphere of intrigue. "Small as I was," he writes, "I was accused of being a spy, etc, etc.,"[5] for his family spoke German. Spy or not, during these years the boy's creative and aesthetic inclinations became manifest.

Even before, in Wisconsin, one is aware of a solitary child content with a world of his own imagination. The garden enthralled him, and the story is told that, when his silence inspired his mother to call to ask what he was doing, he would reply, "*Blümenpficken.*" There were fewer flowers to pick in Texas, but, prodded perhaps by his sister Gertrude, he took an interest in dancing. Amusingly, since he was smaller than his sister he had to dance the part of Eurydice to her Orpheus; but he did so unflinchingly and, from all reports, with grace. A family snapshot at this time shows him to have been a handsome and well-knit youngster dressed in an outlandish costume which contrasts with his serious mien; he is shown dancing with his sister. At this same time he began also to take an amateurish interest in painting.

When in 1920 the family moved to Bryn Mawr, where he attended high school, he became fascinated for a time with creating puppet shows. He wrote the plays, made the costumes and scenery. Some of the plays were given as entertainments to Bryn Mawr faculty members. No doubt all of this was captivating. Yet one pauses to observe that youngsters who, like the Brontë children, create little fantastic cosmogonies are lonely children. Their superiority, despite any love lavished on them, creates the loneliness. Frederic Prokosch in adolescence was as lonely and shy as the heroes in his novels. Even when he speaks about the two years spent abroad before entering college, studying and traveling in Europe and western Asia, he remarks upon his "general loneliness."[6]

But his matriculation at Haverford College wrought changes. His sister remembers that his reticence gave way to "sociability." The reasons for the change are embedded in the novel A Ballad of Love. Primary among these is the fact that he became an excellent athlete, particularly in tennis and squash; and he began, perhaps without great seriousness at first, to write poetry. The physical sport gave him something hard and purely objective to pit himself against. Like all happy physical activity, it turned the personality out toward the world. At the same time the formal demands, the self-knowledge of poetry gave him a hard and focused center within. Both poetry and tennis command and develop symmetry, and symmetry is the essence of happiness, whether of body or soul.

Court games remained an enthusiasm with Prokosch long after leaving college. He won several competitions in tennis in America, Baden-Baden, and in Mallorca. In squash, he held the championship of Connecticut in 1933, the national championship of France in 1939 and of Sweden in 1944. He looked upon these court games as being akin to aesthetic experience, associating them with gentility and ceremony. When in the mid-1930's he wrote a little piece on the Wimbledon matches, he regretted the commercialization of the meet; but he felt that Wimbledon still continued to encourage the decorum of a European tradition —a tradition about to disappear.[7] Somewhat wistfully in 1962 he wrote: "I used to be a fine athlete: Now I catch butterflies (I did it as a child too—long before I ever heard of Nabokov— and my specialty is tropical butterflies, unlike Nabokov)."[8]

As to poetry, he must have written a good deal while at Haverford; for in 1927, the year after his graduation at the head of his class, his poems began to appear in journals. His first important publication in the July, 1927, issue of the *Virginia Quarterly Review* reposes alongside a contribution by Allen Tate, as an example, in the editors' opinion, of avant-garde verse. For nearly twenty years afterward, his poems appeared regularly in magazines in America and England. In 1940 he was awarded *Poetry* magazine's Harriet Monroe Prize for lyrical poetry.

However, when Prokosch received a master's degree from Haverford in 1928, he had not as yet settled on a career as a writer. Scholarship to the brilliant student made a serious appeal, and he accepted a research fellowship at the University of Pennsylvania in 1929. The next year he attended King's College, Cambridge, as an honorary research fellow, again receiving the master's degree. He returned to America for further graduate study at Yale University, receiving his doctorate in 1932. The topic of his thesis, "The Chaucerian Apocrypha," has been described as being "as far as imaginable from the creative work he was shortly to do."[9] The title is traditionally Germanic, but Prokosch, it should be remembered, was interested ·in the true Chaucer as well as in the apocryphal Chaucers.

In Chaucer he perceived a method of narration which is strangely like his own. In an essay published in 1936, one year after the publication of his first novel, he considers *Troilus and Criseyde* as an example of the art of fiction. Among other things he observes that Chaucer's story moves by "flashes of detail": "In fact, the very onrush seems to consist to a large degree of a pretty leaping from here to there, sudden bursts of energy and affection, changeableness . . . The very changefulness effects a melting together—affection and sarcasm, intimacy and aloofness—all elements flow together and produce an odd quivering liveliness and loveliness, like that of a rippling stream that springs over sand, over pebble, through sunlight and shadow. It eludes us; the taste vanishes as soon as the tale is ended." A bit later on in the essay he speaks of Chaucer's tendency to shift focus: "Now sharp . . . , now remote, vague and misty; now external, objective, derogatory; now within the heart, subjective. . . ." He further submits that the "technique of shift tends to create an effect of nervousness, of restlessness" and that the shift of focus achieves "a peculiarly delicate harmony, a conjunction of echoes."[10]

Outside of any concern as to whether Prokosch is right or wrong about Chaucer, or whether he is reading himself into Chaucer, he clearly felt a confirming support for some of his own fictional techniques. One may even wonder if the scholarly concern with medieval literature was entirely antithetical to Prokosch's creative interests. Whatever the case, an urge to write fiction in addition to poetry accelerated during this time.

While working for his doctorate and for a year afterward, Frederic Prokosch taught English at Yale (1931-1933), continuing in 1934 as a research fellow. From 1936 to 1937 he was an instructor of English at New York University. At Yale he had the reputation of being a very dramatic teacher. And he appears to have led a rather dashing life, maintaining a large yellow convertible and a German shepherd dog. There is also just a suggestion that he was rankled by the pressures of preparing for classes and of grading papers.

While at Yale he wrote a novel, never to be published, which, according to his sister, was rather conventional in its characterization and movement. He also wrote his first published novel *The Asiatics*. It is noteworthy that two sections of *The Asiatics* were published as stories, one in *Scribner's* and another in Whit Burnett's fine old *Story*—noteworthy for the implication that *The Asiatics* was conceived as small, relatively complete units rather than as a single, grand plan.

III *Year of Fame*

An episodic novel, *The Asiatics* (1935) records an impromptu journey from Beirut to Hong Kong, with pauses in Turkey, Iran, India, and French Indo-China. The narrator is a young American who drifts in and out of various experiences such as smuggling opium, crashing in an airplane, making love, and discussing philosophy. As to the genesis of the novel, Prokosch once wrote somewhat cryptically:

> I rather suspect that you'd like to know whether *The Asiatics* is "autobiographical." Well, a part of it is, of course, but most of it isn't. It's called a novel, and that is precisely what it is, and furthermore it is a novel in a well-established (if at the moment —due possibly to the plethora of actual autobiographies—a somewhat neglected) tradition. French literature, and English too, is full of picaresque novels of precisely this type, e. g. Voltaire, Montesquieu, d'Urfe, Mme. de Scudery . . . Fielding, Defoe, Swift. The list could be prolonged indefinitely, and it includes much of the most exquisite in literature, i.e., tales of adventure, "exotic" perhaps, "fantastic," possibly, tho frequently grounded in certain actual experiences, events strung together like beads on a chain without the insistence on a plot in the modern sense (which dates back no further than Richardson), and attaining unity not thru a uniformity of setting or personages but rather thru an individuality of outlook, say; of meditation and of imagination.
>
> I believe all of the Asiatics is quite accurate, geographically and socially speaking, with two very minor exceptions which will be corrected in the seventh edition.[11]

This statement does not reveal much beyond the fact that the young man had recently received a doctoral degree. But the last sentence, with its worry about geographic and sociological accuracy, is significant. It suggests that the novel was "researched." It apparently was, for his sister says that, prior to writing *The Asiatics,* he had travel books scattered all over his room. Only Cyril Connoly has had the temerity to offer a source by wondering if one of the characters in *The Asiatics* might not be based on the rajah in J. R. Ackerley's *Hindoo Holiday* (1932).[12] The guess, so far as similarity between the characters goes, is not bad; but, in the absence of proof, one is tempted less to think of specific sources than of a blending of many.

That geography always fascinated Prokosch is suggested by the numerous examples in his novels of characters drunk with place names. One may particularly adduce a paragraph from *A Ballad of Love* where the hero tells of his childhood: "But my greatest interest lay in geography. I stared at maps by the hour. I fell in love with multitudinous little corners of the world. As I drew my finger along the wrinkled black line of a coast or a river, tempestuous landscapes rose before me—the reedy stretches of Patagonia, the crystal domes of the Aleutians, the poisonous thickets of Sarawak" (p. 59).

The Asiatics with its mirage-landscapes, its ambush of alien faces, its strange coupling of doom and amusement, both puzzled and captivated its audience in 1935. The novel was entirely different from the confessional of Thomas Wolfe or from the awkward social documentary of Sinclair Lewis and Theodore Dreiser. It was different, too, from the neurotic localism of Sherwood Anderson or from the tragic, experiential narrative of Ernest Hemingway. Not even the minor strain of exoticism embodied in such novels as Hilda Doolittle's *Hedylus* (1928) or Thornton Wilder's *The Women of Andros* (1930) had anything in common with the tone of *The Asiatics*. Certainly, such historical centos as Pearl Buck's *The Good Earth* (1931) and Hervey Allen's *Anthony Adverse* (1933) are of a different order from Prokosch's. And James Branch Cabell's romanticism was too arch and disillusioned to remind one of *The Asiatics*. No, Frederic Prokosch's first novel was and is unique. Any attempt to suggest parallels or sources inspires only a convulsion of disbelief.

That the depression-weary readers of the mid-1930's found in the novel a means of escape is unquestionably true and may help to account for its popularity. If so, it would not be the first time that a novel has been acclaimed for the wrong reasons. However that may be, *The Asiatics* was not only a success in America but also an international one. In a short period of time translations were available in the major European countries, and *The Asiatics* was eventually translated into seventeen different languages.[13] Nearly thirty years after its first appearance, *The Asiatics* is still in print in America.

Critical applause accompanied the popularity. Mark Van Doren, Cyril Connoly, Pearl Buck, and Joseph Wood Krutch wrote in praise of the book. Among Krutch's observations, however, was a demurral prophetic of later proscriptions: "The only real question," he wrote, "is the question how deeply the thing is really felt, how much of what he says springs from anything deeper than a sort of luxurious green sickness."[14]

Prokosch could not have been concerned with any sickness, green or otherwise, at this moment of early success. He returned to Europe in 1935, picking a bit once again at the pseudo-Chaucerian manuscripts at Cambridge University, but scholarly ambition had been challenged by the possibility of making his way as a novelist. He must also in England at this time have become aware of the European tradition of the man of letters, the intellectual who survives by right of being a literate spokesman. He knew at this time the English poets W. H. Auden, Stephen Spender, Cecil Day-Lewis, and followers of this triumvirate. That he was less than totally dedicated to scholarship is suggested by his writing from Paris in March, 1936, that he had recently skirmished about a bit in northern Africa and western Asia. "In a few days I shall take a long Balkan journey, and dash up to visit Bukhara and Samarkand as well."[15] True, he returned to teach at New York University for the 1936-37 term, but in 1936 he published his first volume of poems and by the end of 1937 he had received a Guggenheim award, and his second novel had been chosen as the Harper Prize Novel, bringing an award of $7,500. The academic career was abandoned forever.

The Assassins (1936), Prokosch's first collection of poems, published by Chatto and Windus in England and by Harpers in America, shows the poet in a state of vernal potential. The poems engage the reader with a lyric turn that, at its best, effects a union of spontaneity and discipline. An admiration of William Butler Yeats is noticeable, and Yeats's own reaction to the poems must have deeply pleased Prokosch: "Mr. Prokosch's poetic gift is one which strikes me as, considering the time and place, astonishing. It is rich and immediate, musical always; the talent of a real visionary, and often magical."[16] Inasmuch as Yeats's words have been misquoted and made to apply to *The Asiatics* rather than to *The Assassins* in one standard reference work and in

Richard Carpenter's essay "The Novels of Frederic Prokosch," this is as good a time as any to set the record straight.

In general, the reviews of the poems were favorable. There was enough of formal beauty in them to compel the admiration of Michael Roberts[17] and of the poet Edwin Muir[18] in England. There was enough flavor of cyclic change and doom to interest Robinson Jeffers whose poem "Rock and Hawk" Prokosch had privately published at Yale in 1934. Jeffers wrote: "There are lines that express more truth about contemporary history than many whole volumes of recent political comment."[19] John Peale Bishop, who reviewed *The Assassins* for *Poetry, a Magazine of Verse*, also dwelt upon the "Spenglerian" tone and concluded that the poet was worth both watching and reading.[20]

Prokosch's second novel *The Seven Who Fled* (1937) was selected from over six hundred manuscripts for the Harper Novel Prize by a panel of judges consisting of Louis Bromfield, Sinclair Lewis, and Thornton Wilder. *The Seven Who Fled* spills seven Europeans into the heart of Asia and follows their separate symbolic journeys toward destiny. Exploiting the earlier success of mood and setting and, within the separate stories adding a firmer structure, the novel added to Frederic Prokosch's rising reputation. Alfred Kazin found the book "a distinguished novel that is not only an uncommonly beautiful book of prose, but a document of and for our times."[21] But if the reception was enthusiastic, there were, among the reviewers, doubts about meaning. And Mary McCarthy intensely disliked the book: "The characters . . . have so little personal identity, so little individual clearness of tone, that the novel in the end reduces itself to a catalogue of the author's sensations, the author's private confession."[22]

Prokosch himself at this time was less likely to be disturbed by occasional strictures than by the pitfalls of a sudden and enormous popularity. Not, of course, that he was not elated. But he sensed the dangers. He left New York University and traveled abroad, writing in 1937 from Prague that his chief interests were "tennis, squash, baroque architecture, the Greek Islands, medieval Latin poetry, and trying to avoid the vulgarizations of money and publicity."[23] The ambition to avoid these vulgarizations is in retrospect ironical; for, though his reputation was to hold for another few years, it was destined in America at least to decline to near oblivion after 1945.

The grounds for this decline were available if not obvious in the receptions of his second volume of verse and of his third novel. The poems included in *Carnival* (1938) evidence a shift in technique from a youthful sweetness toward a somewhat lithic staticity. *Night of the Poor* (1939), though it sold well and even received some absurdly high praise, is one of his poorest novels. Set in depression-ridden America and involving the journey of a penniless seventeen-year-old boy from Wisconsin to Texas, it reads like a shot-gun marriage between Rand McNally and John Steinbeck. Mark Schorer, who immediately put his finger on the trouble, observed that it is "a book which falls squarely between the fantastic and the prosaic. This is a curious and unsatisfactory state of affairs."[24] Similarly, Clifton Fadiman saw that the novel had "misfired," but he found that it did "not alter" his "conviction that Mr. Prokosch is one of the important younger novelists of the land."[25]

Looking back, one might add that the novel's real failure is that Prokosch attempted to do something for which he had no talent: all his alliances, all his sensibilities are aristocratic; but he tried bravely, though foolishly, to handle ordinary, folksy characters. He was never so brave nor so foolish again. At the same time one must also observe that he was trying in *Night of the Poor* to break away from the Asian formula of his earlier novels; to change, in other words, without losing his identity. This attempt he continued, though in a different, more successful way, in his fourth novel.

Between *Night of the Poor* and *The Skies of Europe* (1941) Prokosch published his third volume of poems, *Death at Sea* (1940). The poems in *Carnival* had moved in the direction of a kind of loaded understatement and even of flatness; this third collection went further in the same direction. It did not fare well. Kinder than most reviewers, Kathleen Raine coolly remarked that "His are verses that any editor could publish without embarrassment, and any critic read without pain."[26] Randall Jarrel found Prokosch "a sort of decerebrate Auden."[27] And

Louise Bogan, whose criticism always tastes as if it had been concocted in a Schrafft's Restaurant, found that the "real hunger,
rage, analysis, terror, observation and tragic pathos which mark
a poet of first and obvious rank are not in him. But he sounds
very soothing."[28]

The tragic fact is that Prokosch had worked hard on his poems.
The later ones, it is true, do not have the immediate, sprinting
excitement of the earlier poems. Yet, if they do not sprint,
they are well paced for the middle distances and are, all
told, better, more solid performances. It is not, therefore, totally
surprising that, disgusted by the American reviews, he vowed
never again to publish poetry in this country.[29] The vow was
not strictly observed, but Prokosch has written very little new
poetry since 1940. Perhaps the failure of *Death at Sea* narrowed
his aims and committed him more absolutely to being a
novelist.

The Skies of Europe (1941), because it confines itself to
relatively realistic characters in relatively real situations, comes
as a surprise. On the surface it is a story of a love that is almost
but not quite disastrous; beneath the surface it is a document of
the antecedents of World War II. And further down it is a somber allegory of the artist—an allegory which ultimately syn-
thesizes the personal and historical aspects of the story. The
scene shifts restlessly from its center in Paris to other places in
Europe, but it does not follow the formula of the Asiatic
travelogue. Behind the creation of *The Skies of Europe* stands a
decision which, though formed gradually, suddenly crystallized
and became crucial.

Frederic Prokosch's life had been cosmopolitan. His sympathies
had never been confined to a particular mode of manners nor
to a particular region. Furthermore, in his most susceptible
years he had become aware, along with most intellectuals, of
the price of nationalism in Europe and of its reverse counter-
part, isolationism in America. In *The Skies of Europe* he brought
together his personal internationalism with the public plea for
political internationalism. He saw evidence that the historical
American isolationist policy had begun to dissipate after war
broke out in Europe,[30] and he felt that literature itself should

contribute to breaking down the walls between nations. He thus set a serious goal for himself as a writer:

> My greatest desire is to take part, however humbly, in the resurrection and growth of a truly international literature—an approach to writing which exceeds national limitations, both in matter and mentality. Such an approach alone seems to me to promise a real imaginative and intellectual maturity for our time, as well as offering the hope of uniting, more firmly, our literature in America to the social forces of the years to come. America has already made great contributions to such a literature; and she is, both by nature and circumstance, the land now best equipped to nourish its growth and its healing influence.[31]

The aim of this credo—that of bringing an American sensibility to a literature which sought to transcend national boundaries—Frederic Prokosch pursued in almost all his novels written after 1940. Prokosch's international intent, however, has usually been missed or ignored, as it generally was in the reception of *The Skies of Europe*. Even so, his reputation was enhanced by this novel and reached its highest point with the publication of *The Conspirators* in 1943.

Prokosch was well prepared to write this story of international intrigue and espionage set in war-time Lisbon; he spent the year after the fall of France in Portugal and knew at firsthand the swarms of refugees and political agents who flocked to Lisbon. The most restricted as to time, plot, and action of Prokosch's novels, *The Conspirators* relates with fine suspense the discovery and assassination of a Nazi agent; but its purpose of delineating the psychic deforming of all conspirators rises above the melodrama.

In 1944 Warner Brothers produced *The Conspirators* as a motion picture, which starred Hedy Lamarr and Paul Henreid and was directed by Jean Negulesco. The adaptation was drastic. The hero was converted into a super-spy known as "the Flying Dutchman." Despite a handsome production the film was rather logy if not actually dropsical.[32] Like many a novelist, Prokosch was scarcely exultant over the production. Indeed, far from elated, he wondered if Hollywood were not "truly moribund."[33]

IV *Decline of Reputation*

When America entered the war, Frederic Prokosch returned to the United States to enter government service in the Office of War Information. In 1943 he was attached to the American legation in Stockholm. His duties seem to have consisted largely of using Stockholm as a listening post in order to develop sources of information. Near the end of the European phase of the war, *Age of Thunder* (1944) appeared. This novel seriously damaged his reputation. Edmund Wilson called the book "a high grade phoney."[34] Wilson may have gone too far, but the book is uneven. The dreamy narrative of a young American spy wandering from eastern France into Switzerland was not only too facile but also disastrously out of tune with the passion for absolute realism or absolute escape which war inspires in people.

Nor did *The Idols of the Cave* (1946) do anything to salvage Prokosch's rapidly waning reputation. No more than in *Night of the Poor* was he capable of treating an American scene with sustained fidelity. Since the novel is set entirely in New York City during the war years and is concerned to some degree with European refugees, *The Idols of the Cave* suggests that Prokosch may have been striving to duplicate the success of *The Conspirators*. But if so, one wonders why he also brushed into his canvas an analogue to the love affair in *The Skies of Europe*. *The Idols of the Cave* sags under the weight of too many intentions and too many characters, many of whom are in the last analysis only brittle caricatures.

During the war, Prokosch had written two indifferent novels; and, in the space of three years, he had lost much of his renown in America. His earlier successes as a novelist had depended to some extent on his ability to capture with chilling intensity the sodden despairs and fears of war, despairs and fears which dogged a whole generation. His art was magically attuned to premonition and vague alarm, to suspicion and murmurings of change to come, to births like deaths, and to beasts slouching toward Bethlehem. When his Asiatics or Europeans muttered of a dying world and of some unimaginable future, when they sighed for the lost Age of Reason and contemplated some age

of sterile mechanisms, the reader could agree, feeling that it might be true. The war changed all that. One had to deal with the certainties of time and space as they presented themselves, not with the uncertainties as they might ensue. The war and particularly the results of the war also finally altered Prokosch's own view of the state of the world.

Returning to France and to Italy after the war, he saw that, though Europe was changed, it was not at all dead. "On the shores of the Mediterranean," he wrote, "one feels that Western culture which has gone on for many centuries may not, after all, be poised, in 1948, on the brink of irremediable collapse." While France might still be "a bit neurotic," he found that most of Europe was still alive. And Venice, "the most breathtaking city in the world," reminded him "that much that is old is still cogently vital."[35] Obviously, to one who had built his early fiction on the belief that war would wipe away the ceremony and decorum of Europe's past, these discoveries meant that some change of emphasis would have to take place in his novels. This change did in fact take place.

Meantime Prokosch published in 1947 two translations of poetry and a selection of his own poetry. He had previously published in 1943 a translation of some of Hölderlin's poems in the New Directions pamphlet series of "The Poets of the Year." To this he added a translation of the *Love Sonnets* of the six-teenth-century French poetess Louise Labé as well as a transla-tion of Euripides' *Medea*. His own *Chosen Poems* (1947) was greeted with respect but not much enthusiasm. Babette Deutsch's reaction is typical: "His verse suffers from a tendency to become verbose, literary, soft and damp. This is the more regrettable because Mr. Prokosch is a sensitive and gifted lyricist, perfectly aware of the moral failure and anguish that are the hallmarks of the age."[36]

V *The Later Phase*

In 1948 he published *Storm and Echo*, the first of the novels which reflect a veering toward optimism for the future of civilization. The central African setting and the hero's search for a spiritually gifted European who has disappeared in the heart of darkness inevitably call Joseph Conrad to mind. The novel is Prokosch's most difficult to understand, for it represents his altered beliefs in a stage of agonized transition. However, the note of hope, the hint that a grand and continually evolving civilization is man's destiny, whether man likes it or not, is clear. *Storm and Echo,* where the echoes are the retreating reverberations of the spiritual storm of the war, is perhaps the only novel of Prokosch's to which one feels tempted to apply the term "powerful." It deserved a better critical reception, but it had committed the sin of baffling its readers.

On the occasion of the publication of his ninth novel, *Nine Days to Mukalla,* Prokosch returned briefly in 1953 to America. He had criticisms of his country. The young writers, he felt, wanted "the rewards without the trials and struggle." He found that the writers were paralleled by the youth in America whom he saw, in general, as "pampered, lacking in conviction, without fire." Still, he saw a "good side: the sense of things changing, of potentiality, of possibilities."[37]

His new novel *Nine Days to Mukalla* (1953) to a degree embodied these observations. Like *Storm and Echo, Nine Days to Mukalla* struck his most profitable vein, that of a symbolic journey through a symbolic land of hardship and demonic beauty. As in other of his novels, the destiny of most of his characters—derelicts of a plane crash in Arabia—is death. These deaths, however, implement an allegorical theme that is both psychological and historical. That the allegory is subtle is indicated by the fact that no reviewer was aware of it. Unaware of its theme, few reviewers recognized that the novel was in certain ways as distinguished as Prokosch's highly praised early novels.

Among the few, Gore Vidal, then at the height of his meteoric success as a novelist, wrote: "At his best, as in this work, he writes a rich evocative line with which he creates sensuous worlds he has never seen except with the eye of a superlative imagination."[38] And that sound, learned critic, Howard Mumford Jones, finding that Prokosch sometimes wrote on the level of Conrad, ranked the book as belonging stylistically "with his best," adding that Prokosch "is a sort of Berlioz of prose."[39] Philip J. Scharper, writing for *Commonweal,* a magazine that has always considered reviewing a serious matter, commented:

"One is happily aware that he is reading the work of an unfortunately rare type—the novelist who seriously regards his medium as a fine art and is not afraid to meet its challenge."[40]

Prokosch has said of his numerous sojourns in Europe and of a year spent after the war in Hong Kong that such travels did nothing for his writing beyond confirming his cosmopolitan viewpoint. Nevertheless, the years 1947-53 spent in Italy, and the year 1951-52 as a Fulbright Fellow at the University of Rome, seem to have had some direct bearing on his tenth novel, *A Tale for Midnight* (1955). For he went through the material in the Vatican Library about the sinister Renaissance Cenci family. And he discussed the material with one of the century's truly great men, George Santayana. In *A Tale for Midnight* Prokosch refashioned the story of the sixteenth-century Roman nobleman, Francisco Cenci, murdered by his daughter Beatrice who claimed that her father had forced her into incestuous relations. The story, which inspired Shelley's drama *The Cenci* (1820), contains obvious opportunities not only for melodrama but also for psychological insight. Employing a cool prose and a simplified syntax for his one historical novel, Prokosch seemed primarily content with creating a story. The novel, well received, went into several printings.

Five years lapsed before another novel appeared. In *A Ballad of Love* (1960), Prokosch gathered together strands he had used in previous novels. The innocence of a Wisconsin boyhood, used in *Night of the Poor;* the calamitous love affair with a woman constitutionally incapable of fidelity, used in *The Skies of Europe* and in *The Idols of the Cave*—these ideas once again rise before the reader's eyes. The effect is often one of a cluttering and dissipation of force. While *A Ballad of Love* is of extreme interest in the evolution of Prokosch's attitudes, it does not add to his stature.

But just as one might have thought Prokosch's career had petered out in trivial repetitions, his latest novel *The Seven Sisters* (1962) compels astonishment at his fertility. For the first time in his career Prokosch has been able to touch American settings with the same delicate magic as he had those of Europe, Asia, and Africa. For the first time he has been able to distil the spiritual truth of American landscapes. Like *The Seven*

Who Fled, the novel follows the stories of separate characters to their ultimate and fatal shaping. At times scene and mood ascend to breathtaking altitudes. So strangely highlighted is the reality that the supernatural scenes seem natural.

Unhappily, this remarkable achievement arrived at a time when Prokosch had been consigned to a critical pigeonhole and was not taken seriously. He is thought of today as one who writes travelogues, who does a nice job of describing places and whose work should be dutifully reviewed by third-rate reviewers—perhaps that pleasant assistant professor who could use an item in his bibliography. And yet, against this impression of Prokosch's worth must be set the opinions of some of the greatest writers of the century. In addition to Yeats, three other winners of the Nobel Prize for literature saw important promise in Prokosch's work. Of *The Asiatics*, André Gide wrote: "An astonishing feat of the imagination. Poetic in its sensuality, witty in its melodrama, urban in its misanthropy, incandescent in its imagery: it is unique among novels and an authentic master-piece."[41] In a similar mood Thomas Mann called *The Asiatics* "A book which has stimulated, haunted and enthralled me. For days I was unable to tear myself away from this astonishing picaresque romance, flashing with talent and an audacious, adventurous spirit. I count it among the most brilliant and original achievements of the young literary generation."[42]

Such comments are not limited to *The Asiatics*, for Albert Camus wrote as follows about Prokosch's career: "He has invented what might be called the geographical novel, in which he mingles sensuality with irony, lucidity with mystery. He conveys a fatalistic sense of life half-hidden beneath a rich animal energy. He is a master of moods and undertones, a virtuoso in the feeling of place, and he writes in a style of supple elegance."[43] And even such a dubious performance as *A Ballad of Love* evoked praise from Somerset Maugham and Thornton Wilder. Moreover, Marianne Moore wrote of it: "The wonderful selectiveness, the allure, the judgment with which the use of the sophisticated alternates with averageness, preserving the verity: consummate!"[44]

What does all this mean? Does it mean that the reviewers are all fools? Does it mean that great writers, who are often very bad critics, have merely been easily taken in? The answer to both questions is *no*. The responses of Yeats, Gide, Mann, Camus, and Marianne Moore indicate that Prokosch's work contains artistic triumphs which a fine artist can immediately perceive to be enormously difficult to achieve. As to reviewers, they discriminate almost always for the moment, for the day's fashion; they scarcely ever legislate permanently. They serve an immediate, temporary purpose.

But the judgment of temporary fashion is no longer useful in evaluating Prokosch's work, nor is it fair. His twelve novels now exist in a relationship both with each other and their time. As they echo back and forth among themselves, they create a body of work which has evolved and advanced over a period of nearly thirty years. No reviewer could ever completely understand one of the later novels without comprehending the whole career, the whole body of work, the whole literary personality. To the end of comprehending the whole, the remaining chapters of this study are dedicated.

However, because of the limitations of space, these chapters cannot do full justice to the poetry. Assuming that Prokosch's primary commitment has been to fiction, the approach largely concerns itself with the matters that reviews of the novels have neglected: the forms, the themes, the meanings. Chronology has been ignored for the sake of considering together those novels which possess common grounds. I admit that other groupings are possible. My own somewhat arbitrary configurations seek to demonstrate the range of Frederic Prokosch's art: the novel of spiritual vagabondage; the novel of the artist in a decadent world; the novel of historical portent; and, most important of all, the novel of individual destiny.

CHAPTER 2

The Poetry: An Analytical Note

I The Assassins

FREDERIC PROKOSCH began publishing poems in American periodicals when in his early twenties. Not all of these poems were reprinted in subsequent books, and perhaps for a good reason. Not that the youthful efforts were bad, but, even though they impressed some editors as being daring, they do not seem now to have much individuality. And whatever else one may say about Prokosch's later, mature poems, they do, at their best, possess a recognizable voice that sings louder than the other voices of evident influences in his poetry.

Fortunately, and surprisingly for a quite young poet, the influences are multiple in his first collection. He is not engulfed by some primary, overpowering voice, so that even in the beginning, his poems do not labor under a single mentor but preserve some idiosyncrasy in the presence of tutors. And the range of influence is as interesting as the multiplicity.

The most immediate, most recognizable influences are of the least importance. They are those of Edna St. Vincent Millay and of Archibald MacLeish. Millay is discoverable in a tendency to pack the last lines of certain poems with an emotive conclusion. MacLeish, a more obvious and persuasive mentor, is found in Prokosch's tendency to reproduce the long diurnal saunter of time and space which MacLeish brought to such a stunning success in his poem "You, Andrew Marvell." Such poems seem to turn inevitably to a heavy use of the conjunction "and," finding it appropriate to the fluid concept of time and to the linking of continents of detail. The illusion of a continuum of time is preserved by avoiding the absolute stops of periods. By way of illustration, in Prokosch's poem, "The Voyage," fifteen of the twenty-four lines begin with the word "and":

> Felt the wild-eyed longing among the enormous
> sea-birds
> And the silvery listening to rhythm of ocean rise
> And the shattering under the cliffs that shadow
> the ruins
> And the ague of the whitened flesh in the starlit
> house and the whitening eyes . . .
>
> (45)[1]

The poet's fascination here with such effects of drift and association doubtless reflects not merely an awareness of MacLeish's poetry but also a personal obsession with motion and restless change—one which also characterizes his novels.

Profounder influence comes from the German Romantic poet Friedrich Hölderlin (1770-1843) and from William Butler Yeats. Their effect is not confined to gesture—which is as far as the effects of Millay and MacLeish go—but permeates the first volume of poems. Moreover, their effect never quite disappears. Friedrich Hölderlin, despite his thematic philhellenism, had some basic common ground with Wordsworth. He was continuously homesick for his youth. He felt that some earlier imaginative rapport with nature had forever gone from his life. He held, however, that, on the foundations of these ashes, arose a belief in "life" or "humanity." These ingredients are the main characteristics of Wordsworth's best poems. From such a base, therefore, in his poem *Sokrates und Alkibiades*, Hölderlin poses the question as to why "holy" Socrates should look with love on Alcibiades, "just a boy." The answer for Hölderlin is that the deepest thinker will love the "livingest" thing, and wise men will ultimately love not abstractions of the mind but beauty in the flesh.

Prokosch very obviously remembers *Sokrates und Alkibiades* in his own poem "The Fishermen," but his intent is to draw attention not to the way of the wise, but to the frenzy of love:

> Do you recall that wise one, the misshapen,
> Whose eyes fell on the fluttering chlamys, and love
> Burned in the whitehot core
> Of wisdom? And the hemlock?
>
> (69)

On the other hand, Prokosch does not possess a noticeably Romantic faith in childhood, nor does he find nature either good or evil; and in these preliminaries he differs materially from a Hölderlin or a Wordsworth. Still, like them, sensing his exile from youth and nature, he turns to a compensatory belief in humanity. In generalizing this pattern, one can say that at bottom such poets, ceasing to place faith in the past and in environment, come to believe primarily in the present and in the self.

Hölderlin's rhythms, more than his concepts, affected Prokosch's poetry. Hölderlin tended to try to produce in accentual German the effect of Greek alcaics or the Asclepiadean meter. Outside the problem of success or failure of the experiment, the attempt appears to have enforced in Hölderlin a tendency toward a slowing of the line toward its end. (In large measure the impression of a decrescendo results from the reader's anticipating an iamb or trochee and from his getting instead an approximation of a spondee.) Something of the same effect appears frequently in Prokosch's long lines which slide often to sixteen syllables. This lengthening imparts to Prokosch's verse a slightly archaic flavor, although the flavor is not that of classical antiquity but of a muted and domesticated Anglo-Saxon rhythm. The problem of Hölderlin's effect is complicated by the fact that doubtless Prokosch was encouraged in a classical background not only by his family environment but by the kind of disciplines encouraged by Haverford College at the time he attended.

The problem is further complicated by the fact that something of William Butler Yeats's music may also be found in Prokosch's poetry. But with Yeats it is less a matter of a specific quality than that the poetry tends to be so straightforwardly musical, the very quality which Yeats admired in Prokosch's verse. The poem "The Dolls," among Prokosch's earlier poems and still among his best, furnishes an example of his musical gift.

> I found them lying on the shore,
> Sweet shapes, pearl-lipped and crescent-eyed:
> Night after night their hands implore
> Pathetic mercies at my side.

> They reach into my secret night
> With pale and terrifying arms
> And offer in a dark delight
> Their subtle suicidal charms,
>
> . . . .
>
> They are the children of desire,
> They live on fear, they are my deep
> And buried thoughts with eyes of fire,
> They are the furies of my sleep.
>
> (6)

One perceives in "The Dolls" that the commitment is less to meaning than to song. One could possibly distil a psychological resolution from the quatrains, but to do so would be to abuse the poem. Its delight comes from a use of rhyme which is as mysterious as the events in a fairy tale yet just as inevitable. While Yeats's directions are rather different from Prokosch's, many of Yeats's lyrics, particularly the earlier ones, use form in the same way: as a weapon, really, which overpowers the reader before he has a chance to ask vulgar questions about content.

Even though *The Assassins* contains many poems oriented toward places and journeys—roughly one-third of the titles connote a place or a voyage—they follow a lyrical inspiration. Prokosch "sings" about places. Far from describing or explaining, he builds his images toward mood. As an example, in his poem "Port Said" we find these lines no more, no less tantalizing and retreating than any of the others:

> . . . the negroes singing
> Of trouble, and beside them standing
> Those with the long white hands
>
> Not male not female shaping the sign of Hermes:
> Below, the expecting gorge: above, their eyes
> Like pearls in the shell-white faces, thinking
> "Can it
> Be hard to die, is death
> A gentle lover?"
>
> (47)

The poem, largely through connotation and image, evokes a feeling of decadence and doom—of life in death. And one can associate the hermaphroditic sign of Hermes with such a general atmosphere. But seldom does Prokosch's early poetry do more than sort the beads and string them with an eye for type and size. The poems do not contain meaning; they are a tangent to meaning. The poems do not possess design; they are design. The images, in themselves often strikingly conceived, descend with the curious irrelevancy of the snow which falls in slow motion through liquid in those forever sealed glass paperweights.

These strange, quite beautiful poems made Frederic Prokosch for a time a popular, almost a fashionable, poet. His poems were placed in anthologies, conspicuously in those of Oscar Williams. Of more importance, however, Prokosch influenced the work of one of the most remarkable poets of the century: Dylan Thomas.

Thomas' first poetry was highly synthetic. The poems seem to have begun in vague turmoils which acted like a magnet to attract images. Almost everything that could be attracted seemed usable to the younger Thomas, or of being clipped and shaped for use. The earlier poems were, as a result, often absurdly insincere. His idea of poetic language was often no more serious than taking a well-known idiom or a piece of slang and turning it one hundred eighty degrees. Thus, "Once upon a time" might become "Once below a time." These remarks are intended not as final criticisms of Dylan Thomas' achievement but as observation on the origins of his sullen craft. He was open to all attractions—the metaphysicals, the surrealists, Whitman and so forth. As if he were quicksilver, all metals stuck to him. Among those that stuck were the impressive rhythms of Frederic Prokosch's first volume of poems, along with the curiously suspended quality of Prokosch's images. There is no need to argue this point, which may come as a surprise to many, for Thomas confesses the truth of it. In his letters to Vernon Watkins he mentions "unconsciously" borrowing a phrase from Prokosch's poetry. He also had the habit of including a poem or two of Prokosch's in his public readings.[2]

The discussion of Dylan Thomas has been permitted to run

on because it has a point. What, one asks, did Thomas do to raise his art to its eventual high level? The answer is humiliatingly simple: he learned to focus his vagueness and guilty images upon some kind of abstract belief—a dark Christianity, one might say. Prokosch was, unfortunately, never able to believe in belief, let alone a precise doctrine; and his poetry never had a castle to go to nor a home to come back to.

II   The Carnival

Frederic Prokosch's second volume of poems *The Carnival* (1938) shows evolutions. *The Assassins* had been divided almost equally between poems of a lyric adventure and those which imbued place names with emotions of alarm. The lyric adventure evolved in the second volume into an Audenesque song, and the geography pieces became concerned with the environments of impending war. In short, Prokosch tended to bring the emotions of current history into his lyricism and his landscapes.

The songs, like those of W. H. Auden written in the same period, depend heavily upon the ballad for their effects. The traditional ballad usually suggests, without totally revealing, some suppressed, heroic drama. But in the sophisticated ballads of the late 1930's, whatever is at stake involves not heroic concerns but unheroic ones. They involve ordinary guilts, domestic infidelities, and trivial promiscuities. In the best of them, the guilt and faithlessness are gathered together into the grand treachery of war itself. Such is the case with Auden's well-known lyric "Lay your sleeping head human on my faithless arm." To this poem Prokosch's "Nocturne" bears an obvious resemblance:

> Close my darling both your eyes,
> Let your arms lie still at last.
> Calm the lake of falsehood lies
> And the wind of lust has passed . . .
>
> (13)

Similarly, Auden's "O What is That Sound Which so Thrills the Ear" has some kinship with Prokosch's "Fable" in the menace and acceleration of the closing lines:

And the door is locked and the key is lost
And the gulls lie stiffening in the frost
And the rippled snow is tracked with blood
And my love lies cold in the burning wood.

(7)

These lines also illustrate a frequent gesture of Auden's and Prokosch's poetry: the excessive use of the definite article—*the* door, *the* key, *the* gulls, *the* frost, and so on. The effect of this practice is one of generalizing, of typifying, so that in some of Auden's or Prokosch's poems everything seems to fall into overpowering categories. Often Auden couples his definite article with a particularizing adjective with the result that the phrase is able to claim both individuality and generality. And this accomplishment is quite a trick. In the long run, however, such usage—obviously stemming from T. S. Eliot's poetry—makes for an artificiality, an inflation and inertia. But, if Prokosch has been less successful in choosing particularizing adjectives, he has not fallen into the same effect of dead categories. For his adjectives tend, by and large, to open his phrases to a romantic vista of infinitudes. By way of illustration, here are the terminal phrases of three of his songs: "the blind, eternal night," "the soundless dead," "the unutterable shade."

Aside from the songs, *The Carnival* is remarkable for Prokosch's long, honest poem entitled "Ode." This poem—divided into eight sections and moving from morning to midnight—is a solemn and strangely frank summing up of the poet's first thirty years of life. At the same time the personal autobiography combines with a summation of the flow of human history. The whole second section reads like synopses of certain of his early novels. He speaks of his childhood fascination with fairy tales, of his immersion in athletics, and then of his discovery of learning and European culture. One of the most revealing statements that will ever be made about the novels *The Asiatics* and *The Seven Who Fled* is contained in four lines of "Ode":

Asia once held me: the visual leap through the limitless,
A world all covered with hungers, the threatening swarms
Of the past, migrations, and a belief in the dangerous
Magic of human memory.

(74)

And of "the dangerous magic of human memory," one thinks of the characters in *The Seven Who Fled,* whose past releases a vengeful spirit upon them. The ode also forecasts one of the directions of his later novels, for he writes of feeling the presence of "the Ape" whom he also calls "a shaggy messenger" who enters his civilized house, and which he abstracts as "that Hand" (48). The hand of a gorilla haunts the dreams of characters in *Nine Days to Mukalla.* Indeed, some worry about man's animal past pervades most of Prokosch's novels written after World War II. The worry, however, goes back to the first volume of verse; for in the poem "Alexandria" we find a "dark gorilla" that waits "to clutch traveler. Hug him to earth" (*Assassins,* 7).

Besides illuminating Prokosch's life and his novels, "Ode" stirs up other considerations. Once again, one notes that, formally speaking, the rhythm, with its more or less fourteen syllable lines and a lengthened terminal foot, effects a meter which is approximately classical and unlike anything else in modern poetry except John Peale Bishop's experiments with alcaics. Each line rises and falls like Virgilian hexameter. In respect to content, the ode is also unusual, but not in the sense that it is autobiographical, or even confessional, but in the sense that it is so deliberately and even desperately autobiographical and confessional. Beyond doubt, poetry always contains at least a grain or two of self-revelation, but the more it contains, the more it usually sets about disguising it. And this is quite the most astounding thing about Prokosch's "Ode." There is no disguise whatever.

By nature an ode is a serious poem about a serious subject. But one wonders whether the subject should be so serious as the topic of "my life"? Perhaps only Wordsworth in the "Immortality Ode" or in "Tintern Abbey" was ever so honest. And no sooner does one mention Wordsworth than he sees exactly how dangerous this kind of poem can be for the author. Its danger lies in the fact that it tells all; not an ounce of anything basically important is reserved. When one writes that kind of poem, he is near the end of his poetic career; for the creation of poetry depends always upon a state of believing that one has not made himself entirely clear, that he has not told all. Wordsworth, to be sure, continued to write poetry after he wrote the "Immortality Ode," but he might have written richer poetry later in life had he not written that ode early in life. One cannot avoid the impression that, for Prokosch, his "Ode" is almost a farewell to poetry; for, though his very best poems were yet to be written, he was to produce only one more brief collection.

III Death at Sea

Frederic Prokosch's two finest poems "Sunburned Ulysses" and "The Sand" are found in *Death at Sea* (1940). It is hard to read Homer and think of Ulysses as other than a strong, intelligent man who wanted to get home to Ithaca. It is hard to read Tennyson and think of Ulysses as other than one to whom the continuous journey rather than the destination is important. But perhaps it is after all the contests of mind and flesh, of voyage and destination, which make Ulysses the totally adaptable hero for all who have reconsidered his personality after Homer: Dante, Tennyson, Joyce, Kazanzakis. Had Marcel Proust written about Ulysses he would have sent him forth in a cork-lined submarine. Prokosch's Ulysses represents the hero of irrational destiny. He listens to the song of the sirens and understands:

> Sweat poured from his brown chest.
> Loving the unattainable and forbidden, in love with
> change alone,
> He recognized the frightful necessity in the song of the
> sirens: for he likewise possessed
> Flesh fanned easily into fire, and a heart as hard as
> stone.
>
> (42)

"The Sand" is one of the few objective or impersonal poems Frederic Prokosch has written, but this is not to say that one does not recognize in it his fascinations with movement and a kind of abstract human history. Rather, one recognizes that in this poem Prokosch has no particular axe to grind. "The Sand" belongs in a category with some of Kathleen Raine's poems and with some of Robinson Jeffers' in which one feels that the viewpoint has been confined to a cosmic scientist's view, seeing all the awe, yet impersonally and with no comment beyond what the materials themselves add up to. With remarkably controlled power, Prokosch's poem finishes:

> Eastward, southeastward pass the feverish currents.
> They multiply, beget new races, plant like mussels or
> Sea-anemones brilliant new cities along the shore.
> Sometimes a greater wave arises: humanity
> Is pilloried as the wave pours howling through the land.
> New creatures are begotten, new methods of thinking,
> Loving, hating, enduring, all spring like bubbles from the
> cold, interminable sand.
>
> (50)

If "Sunburned Ulysses" and "The Sand" are among Prokosch's best poems, most of the remaining poems in *Death at Sea* suffer from petulance. Over and over again one has the feeling that war interferes with Prokosch's lovemaking. Unquestionably war has never been kind to lovers, yet to view the monstrous dance of war in such a narrow, even selfish way deforms all. No purpose is served in dwelling on such poems.

IV *Translations*

In addition to translating Hölderlin, Frederic Prokosch also translated the love sonnets of Louise Labé and the *Medea* of Euripides. There is some suggestion, too, that he once may have translated Michelangelo's sonnets, for such a translation is listed in the uncorrected galley proofs of *Chosen Poems* as being "by the same author." The item, however, was removed in the corrected proofs; and there is no record of any publication of the sonnets. It is to be hoped that, if the translations exist, they will find publication; for Prokosch is an excellent translator.

Louise Labé, the sixteenth-century tomboy who is rumored to have fought with the Dauphin's army in the siege of Perpignan, wrote poems of some historical interest. They are a potpourri of motives from Catullus, the Greek Anthology, and Italian love poetry. Prokosch's translation does justice to her oddly blunt yet coy expression. And Prokosch does justice to Euripides as well. His *Medea,* combining prose for the speeches of the characters with poetry for the choral speeches, is scrupulously literal and clear. That Dudley Fitts chose Prokosch's version for inclusion in his *Greek Plays in Modern Translation* is ample attestation to the catholicity of the rendition. If one does not find the daring shifts of Robinson Jeffers' adaptation, neither does one find the absurd prettification and absent-minded slavishness of Gilbert Murray's version. In all of his translations Prokosch appears to have been motivated solely by a desire to handle the materials carefully and honestly. His own statement about his translation of Hölderlin suggests his modesty and intent: "The translations are offered, apologetically, as humble versions of a poetry which uniquely transcends translatability."[3]

V *An Unfinished Talent*

Frederic Prokosch's production of poetry has not been large: fewer than one hundred poems have been printed. Furthermore, the poems, roughly the product of perhaps ten years time, were written for the most part between 1930 and 1940. One can probably not treat his expression, limited both in time and amount, as anything other than a potential. Prokosch's talent for poetry remains an unfinished talent. We do not know, nor does it seem likely that we shall ever know, how he might have ended had he chosen to be a poet rather than a novelist. That he made a choice in favor of prose, though probably with reluctance, seems clear; for the novels have come with regularity, and the poems have not. The choice, whether to write poetry or fiction, no doubt had to be made. Though many writers are attracted to both poetry and prose, few can write both; and only a few seem to have been able to write both at the same time. One thinks of George Meredith. One thinks also of Thomas Hardy who deserted fiction late in life to return to poetry. One thinks of Faulkner, thinking of himself as he wrote his novels as a "failed poet." Poetry, while neither a full-time job nor a remunerative one, nevertheless demands a whole consciousness. If energy is invested in fiction, it must be subtracted from the capacity to write poetry. The aesthetic warmth generated in writing prose almost always satisfies the poetic thermostat as well.

While Prokosch's poetry is flawed by a vagueness which leads to occasional dullness and by an excess of emotional words such as "terrifying" or "frightening," which should almost never be said out loud in poetry, his gift for poetry was still a generous one. One must feel sorry that it was made finally into an adjunct of the novel. But of course that is also the compensation; the novels themselves possess a beauty and prodigality of language stolen from the lyric muse.

CHAPTER 3

The Wanderers

I   The Asiatics

IT MAY WELL BE that one of the achievements of the
twentieth century will some day be seen to be a restoration
of an eighteenth-century curiosity, tolerance, and faith in the
species *Homo sapiens*. Man may yet in this century rescue man
from empire, from mechanistic psychology, and from conde-
scending sociology. If so, future men will look back for the
origins of humanistic rebirth. They will, of course, pause with a
number of pieces of impressive evidence. They may come to
consider Alexis Saint-Léger's *Anabase* (1924) of oblique importance.

Written by a French diplomat of mixed racial origin, *Anabase*
claims the theme of the founding of a new city. Yet much of
this long poem describes a slow, crawling migration through
the desert. It is never a rational poem in the sense of clearly
mapping the journey, but the journey itself, its pulse and
relentlessness, its continuous discovery, its sensuality and mystery
become the dimensions of the poem's life. It stirs in the reader
the not-quite-forgotten ecstasies of the nomad's search, which
at heart is the search for the old yet ever renewed images and
metaphors of existence. It murmurs of racial origin, of things we
can never quite comprehend about life yet must ever seek to
comprehend. Without ever using the catch phrase "dignity of
man," *Anabase* forces us to endorse the worth of human existence
for the reason that it makes us look once again at man himself.
To do so is to share the common ground of a passionate essence
far transcending the difference of race. T. S. Eliot's poem "The
Journey of the Magi" reflects that poet's interest in *Anabase*,

which he translated in 1930. More youthfully exuberant, Frederic Prokosch's first novel is a manifestation of a vision similar to Saint-Léger's.

Although *The Asiatics* (1935) makes some tactical errors, it is, surely, an enchanting and original novel as well as a remarkable performance for a young writer. The novel almost appears to be a conscious attempt to emulate the spirit of the picaresque novel with its episodic lurchings and dubious coincidences. The action takes place sometime in the third decade of this century. A young American, who has been robbed of most of his money, makes his way from Beirut to Istanbul; thence to Iran and Russia; and, finally, to India, Malay, Cambodia, Cochin China, and Annam. No reason for the journey presents itself; he learns nothing very tangible; and, though he makes momentarily intense friendships with a number of people, they disappear as mysteriously as they appear. To be sure, like musical themes in a coda, some show up again toward the end of the novel; but, even so, they are soon again lost. The friendships themselves, whether warm or frightening, mutate always into treacheries or desertions. The people are true nomads who can only be understood in the shimmer of their transience. They are neither types nor individuals. They comment upon life, but they themselves are not part of life. They sometimes seem profound, but they never seem wise. The reader is always aware that they are characterizations rather than persons. And all of this is so because they are utterly rootless. Whether they express an ideal or a cynicism, it is always with the menacing and meretricious glamor of a spiritual promiscuity.

Jailed in Turkey, the narrator suffers such terrible deprivation and degradation along with several other characters that one could only suppose that the bonds between him and his fellow prisoners would be great. Yet when he again meets one of them, the Dutchman de Hahn, at the end of the book, this meeting is much like the myriad encounters with strangers. Or, though the narrator and Dr. Ainger have been in a plane wreck together in Iran, when they meet again under different circumstances neither refers to the plane wreck. Of these and similar re-encounters one asks: what is the justification, what is the purpose?

We must seek the answer in the nameless, twenty-two-year-old narrator. This strange young man has qualities in common with a recurring type of American hero who is found in Hawthorne, Mark Twain, Sherwood Anderson, Hemingway, and others. He offers us a viewpoint of essential naïveté which is compromised but not entirely corrupted by experience. Prokosch's narrator is naïve. He is as much a boy as a man, yet his naïveté is of a rather weary sort. Other characters tell him that he looks young but that his eyes are "old." And we learn that he has—like a later, tired practitioner of the naïve viewpoint, J. D. Salinger's Holden Caulfield—a patch of white in his youthful hair.

Since the naïveté is only slightly tarnished by preciousness and disillusionment, it comes to be seen within the vortex of international complexities as a peculiarly *American* naïveté. At the same time the swarms of Europeans and Asiatics whom the hero meets come to be seen as representatives of subtler, of more experienced, and, finally, of more corrupted races. Over and over again Prokosch's Asiatics remind the reader that Asia is old. By implication the narrator and his country appear young and inexperienced. The boy's inexperience is largely preserved, too, as it is for Huckleberry Finn; for he does not become a participator in the neurotic lives, the wicked vanities, and the cruelties of the other characters. He continuously withdraws from them, though he hardly ever morally judges them. Nor do the other characters pursue him. They find him "nice," but in the end he bores them, of course, for he himself has really nothing to say. Yet his bland neutrality is in the last analysis his most engaging quality; and, for the sake of meaning in the novel, it is of considerable importance.

In some degree all of the people whom the young American meets are committed to a world view, a philosophy which is indistinguishable from their personalities. They possess a character, which the narrator does not. Still to possess a character is in their philosophy the same as being possessed by a character. Hence, their lives in that sense are finished. So that when they speak, they reveal a conception of self, which is often of interest; but the reader must guard against being beguiled into accepting their words as final pronouncements of wisdom. For it is their limitation, their "finishedness" that speaks. For example, Antoine Samazeuilh says towards the end of *The Asiatics*:

Well . . . if there's one thing I've learned it's this, life is neither good nor bad. Life, fate, nature, call it whatever you want, that is to say, the way things happen—all this, I say, has no regard for what we two-legged creatures have decided by a majority vote to call good or bad. That's the truth. I'm not deceiving you. Why not see things clearly? It's not so bad, really, once you get used to it. Rather thrilling, in fact. There's nothing one can't get used to, you know, no matter how frightful. You don't need to be particularly brave, unless, of course, you're more sensitive than the rest (417).

Such vignettes on the nature of life are common in Prokosch's novels; and, were one to read them in Joseph Conrad's fiction, one would be obliged to ponder whether or not the philosophy might be a redaction of Conrad's own beliefs. Not so here. Samazeuilh is a Nietzschean immoralist. His words are relevant to himself alone because they are relative to himself alone. The narrator is entirely aware that Samazeuilh's words are expressions of self rather than of truth. Shortly after this particular speech the narrator thinks to himself: "Yes, he was a fine animal, he was fit, he'd survive. I looked at his heavy cruel lips glowing in the sunlight and wondered why I still liked him so well" (417).

In the final analysis the philosophical commitments give no vitality to characters like Samazeuilh but are a form of death for them. At the same time the narrator remains vital and truly alive by his refusal to submit to philosophies. His wisdom must be a refusal to adopt any "wisdom." By such a refusal he gains an advantage: he becomes the observer *par excellence*. When he enters the holy city of Medesh in eastern Iran, he observes:

Not until we came nearer and nearer, and the pure blue of the minarets and the gold of the greater domes grew vivid at last in the clearing air, not until then did it look convincing, look truly like a place that had anything at all to do with men. . . .

But it's odd. That, of course, is what one feels on approaching a new thing; timidity, mystification, a sort of poetry and surprise which presently evaporates more or less forever. More or less,

I say, for possibly it is this first feeling of remoteness and mystery that is really the closest to the truth; and now and then one can't help gliding suddenly and startlingly back to this first feeling, especially at those dusky moments when one's touching the very things that are closest. One wonders. One doesn't quite understand. But of course the truth is that the intimacy and closeness were all an intricate hoax, an ingenious dream, a subtle but half-hearted mirage.

That is what I thought once I'd entered the city. And so I concluded: don't be strong; don't be alone; don't be proud; it's your only chance ever to understand anything at all. Be fragile, be tender, humiliate yourself, and let the discoloration of dream close in on you. Do that, and oddly enough you'll remain healthy; you'll be yourself; you'll discover the best way to live in this particular most fruitless and tantalizing of possible worlds. The reality becomes a cruel dream while the dream fades into a tender man-made reality (163-64).

This passage directs the reader to two primary elements of Prokosch's work: the humiliation of his observer-narrator-hero and the dreamlike pristinity of the observations themselves. The humiliation is contained in his rejection of strength, his rejection of stoic attitudes, his rejection of solitude—a rejection, then, of the foundations on which the important literary heroes of the century have been based. His narrator is, in short, the antithesis of James Joyce's self-reliant hero, of André Gide's, of Thomas Mann's Nietzschean criminal-hero, or of Hemingway's stoic-hero. He is possibly a little like a Henry James observer who has no moral bias, or like a Marcel Proust observer who has no social bias. Because Prokosch's narrator advances from a position of weakness like a child, he sees things without preconceptions—as if for the first time, as if experience had not fallen into pattern. Everything is suspended in the mystery of phenomena.

Yet, if Prokosch's observer sees with the freedom of a child, much of what he sees is nevertheless tarnished, perverse, epicene. And since the character of the observer is so neutral, the observer tends, in the reader's mind, to become what he observes. The perverse innocent, as Jean Genet too well knows, is a fascinating but frightening creature. Fortunately, in the end the sense of the strange beauty of life triumphs in Prokosch's novels over the wicked obliquities. The sympathetic reader ceases to look for ordinary motivation and allows the poetically detailed scenes to sweep over him like voices from a dream or an oracle. Oddly enough, at the very moment when he ceases to examine very closely, the reader becomes aware that thematic material, if not a specific theme, is fermenting in the heavy compost of *The Asiatics*.

When all the elements of *The Asiatics* are composed, they present a large canvas—like a painting by Hieronymus Bosch—of characters trapped in their own illusions of belief and expectations. The Russian Krusnayaskov, as introspective and self-torturing as Conrad's Razimov in *Under Western Eyes*, can only reveal himself in duplicities because duplicity is his assumption about the nature of life. Mme. de Chamellis' sister, la Comtesse, who can think even in senility only of love, is "from the outside . . . laughable." However, when seen "from the inside, even if only for an instant" she grows "like everyone else into a tragic and terrifying shape" (143). Trapped within themselves, the characters proclaim their introversion and decadence. Indeed, the whole of Asia becomes ultimately a study in decadence: the decadence of the resigned Asiatic, that of the hysterically searching European.

As for the young American, he too seeks, but not for money, love, or intrigue but for something he calls "happiness." Of the Asiatics and Europeans alike he asks the question, "Are you happy?" The answers vary from boastfulness to despair, but none confesses to happiness except two humble characters, a Buddhist monk and an old Chinaman who, like the narrator, stand somewhat aside from the pretensions, the ideological allegiances of life. At the end of the novel the old Chinaman urges the narrator to plunge into a sunlit pool. "Don't be afraid," the old man cries. And though the young man dives in, the reader does not suppose that he dives into the anxious life of the Europeans. He dives, possibly, into some conception of life which is "eager" rather than sensual and which makes him feel "affection," not love. These things, however, make him feel "very happy" (423). Eagerness and affection finally come to contrast thematically with fanaticism and ego.

II Storm and Echo

A nomadic tempo characterizes all of Prokosch's work, but only two others of his novels approach the pure wanderlust of *The Asiatics*. However, these later novels—*Storm and Echo* (1948) and *Nine Days to Mukalla* (1953)—are much more definitely committed to theme. Their theme, at least in extension, once again involves decadence and happiness, but somewhat clarified and strengthened.

Storm and Echo, in the sense of its being a novel set in Africa, was preordained by *The Asiatics*. As de Hahn is dying he soliloquizes:

> . . . Asia, my boy, is the final tragic land. It is the last of the five great continents that we come to. Africa is the beginning, Asia is the end. Africa's the land of birth, Asia the land of death. . . .
>
> We're all Asiatics. . . . We're lost, the race is dying. . . .
>
> The certainties and simplicities of life are things that we've all invented ourselves. They did that sort of thing very well in the lovely eighteenth century. The age of reason. Yes, but when reason goes we've got to fall back on instinct. And do you know what instinct is? It's a wild lion roaming through the jungle with blood on his tongue (409-10).

True enough, Prokosch's Africa bears a relationship of origin to the death of his Asia. How metaphorical, how fatalistic, one says, and how curiously superstitious is the sense of place in Prokosch's work! Yes, and it is therefore quite inseparable from meaning.

In *Storm and Echo* where the mystical journey penetrates into the heart of Africa, the traveler trespasses rather than covers a terrain of nightmare origin and instinct. Such an impression is basic, yet there are complications. The novel opens in the town of Louladongo in French Equatorial Africa where first-person narrator Samuel, is arranging a trip to seek a mysterious Leonard Speght, who is rumored to have gone to "Mount Nagala." Samuel is warned by a chance acquaintance that there are no men in Africa, only wrecks: "Go back to Italy. Read Dante.

Ride in a gondola. Visit the Uffizi. There's plenty left, you know, even now" (4). And so, the novel begins with the impression of modern man's trying to pick up the pieces of human destiny after World War II.

Leonard Speght is not permitted to become very clear in the novel. The reader learns little more about him than what is told in the first chapter: "I knew him in Paris before the war. He'd been a schoolteacher in Kansas, and then a sculptor in Greenwich Village; then an architect in Miami, a professional gambler in Cannes, a restauranteur in St. Tropez, a bookseller in Geneva. One day he left for Africa." Samuel does not know what Speght was looking for: "Gold maybe. Or the great illumination. Or self-destruction, perhaps. God only knows. He was always skating along just on the brink of catastrophe" (4).

Three Europeans join the American: Alessandro, an anthropologist, looking for "secret gods"; Joshua, an entomologist, looking for "secret insects"; and Marius, a mineralogist, looking for "secret metals." With the Negro guides and porters, they constitute a safari of white men who, like the dying de Hahn, have lost their faith in reason, "the lovely eighteenth century," and of black men submerged in an atavistic swamp of instinct.

Prokosch's African landscape, even more brilliantly imagined than his Asian, serves several purposes in the novel. Primarily, as in all of his journey novels, it is a place of trial for civilized man. It ages some characters; more subtly, it merely "changes" others; and some it kills. Thirst, hunger and fever, desert, jungle, and the alpine slopes of Mount Nagalla—all take a more than physical toll. As the civilized characters weaken physically, psychological truths emerge. They become brutish, hysterical, and selfish; but, in the end, the psychic changes and the physical suffering bring to each a spiritual clairvoyance. Alessandro knows his emptiness before he dies, Joshua knows his weakness, Marius knows his violent evil. Samuel alone of the white men reaches the mountain but not because he possesses strength but because he possesses "love" and "hope" and "memory" which "manage to keep the soul alive in this heinous darkness" (268).

For Samuel possesses the same humility and neutrality as the hero of *The Asiatics*. It is not that his strength is as the strength of ten because his heart is pure, but because his not so very pure heart rejects the neurotic generalization, the hysterical abstraction, and waits for wisdom to come to him through the senses. He sees that Africa, beautiful and horrible, strips the white man to the bone: "We had changed, changed incalculably. We were stripped of surface oddities—they had been luxuries after all—and the basic, ungovernable oddities at the root of the soul were exposed. . . . The climate of the Congo was like a powerful X ray which penetrated all disguises and gradually revealed, with fearful clarity, the spiritual skeleton of a man" (208).

What is learned from the powerful X ray? Consistent with the idea of Africa as the "origin" of humanity, origin is the primary concern. All the chapters bear the titles of animals, birds, or insects. The role of the fauna within the chapters varies considerably. Sometimes there is only a brief mention or glimpse of elephant or butterfly. However, as the weight of evidence mounts, the reader recognizes that the purpose of such titles is to reinforce the concept of the origins of human sensibility. Each of the Negroes bears, like a burden as well as a sustainer, a totem identity which indicates the boundaries of his strength and cunning. One, thus, is a frog spirit; others, "hawks, leopards and crocodiles." When they dance, they become their totem animal; and, in so doing, their "ancestral guilt" disappears along with loneliness and weakness. They become beasts "plunged in the bliss and misery of animality" (116).

Samuel himself is given the name of "Sambula" by the blacks in an apparent supposition that the name contains a totem animal. And presumably Sambula experiences an animal salvation when, late in the novel, he evades a rhinoceros by diving into a pool. The pool, unlike the sunny pool in *The Asiatics*, is the very swamp of creation. The slime bubbles with a slow, reptilian vitality. In this gelatinous womb Sambula learns that life has mystic parallels. He sees that this pool in Africa possesses some strange identity with a little lake where he and his father long before had rowed a boat. And so, the animal origin and the civilized end of man momentarily merge. The effect of the realization is that of making Samuel wish desperately to live, though previously he had somnolently drifted through exhaustion and illness "half in love with easeful death."

When one apprehends the "bliss and misery of animality" as

the will to live, one also apprehends that Africa represents, symbolically, the desire to live, as contrasted with the Asiatic symbol of the wish to die. This contrast also involves the death wish of the decadent Europeans who journey toward Mount Nagalla and who are seeking, without any real hope, rejuvenation and salvation. Of course, they fall short of their goal. Their souls have been contoured by World War II. Though it is not specifically mentioned, the nuclear bomb hangs over them and civilization seems lost. Prokosch, through a minor character, an utterly decadent European, calls their time "The Age of Hysteria." The phrase is perhaps not so accurate as Auden's "Age of Anxiety," but the meaning is clearly the same. Against the fears and against the wish for death, Africa, in its symbolic aspect, offers an evasive and terrible hope. It represents survival outside any concern either with a civilized dependence on an age of reason or with a fear of The Age of Hysteria. Africa is a blinding reality.

What may be involved in the blinding reality is suggested in the revery which Africa evokes in Samuel. He dreams of a black bull being led by a procession of "small men with Assyrian features," who "seemed to be praying." The reader is taken back to some African parallel with the bull worship in ancient Crete, with all the decisive implications which Crete has for the origins of civilization. Such dreams, Prokosch tells the reader in a passage which bears evident relationship with the philosophy of Carl Jung, relates the individual to the whole inner life of mankind, "to the whole dark reservoir of human experience." Here "the dreamer becomes the race, the dream becomes the ever-widening net of ancestral memory" (137).

One assumes that this ancestral memory is of great value, for it alone possesses the key to the cryptogram of civilization and therefore knows what steps mankind must take in order to persist. Still, the memory rises only briefly, and the experience is so surrounded by fear that the human mind recoils from it. Indeed, the opposition between the religious, passionate desire to rediscover the totem animal, the origin of the tribe, the ancestral memory, and the civilized fear of doing so appears to be the basic theme of *Storm and Echo*. Each of the civilized pilgrims to Mount Nagalla is motivated by both desire and fear:

the desire and fear are profoundly implied by the mysterious figure of Leonard Speght. The desire and fear are incorporated into Mount Nagalla.

Leonard Speght is referred to as a devil and as a saint, a scoundrel and a genius, a jungle deity and an evil spirit. He has become, one supposes, the tribal god of the villagers of Ougala. Their leader says that the travelers can never take the white man away from them: "He is ours!" This apotheosis of Speght is one in which Samuel finally concurs, for he eventually sees in Speght both the civilized fear and the civilized desire for salvation: "What was the unmentionable burden of guilt that finally sent him out here, that left him no peace, that galvanized, exiled, haunted, twisted, tortured, corroded him?" He answers:

> Fear. Some sort of fear, of course. And the courage derived from fear, which became an insatiable appetite for splendor—a dark, evil splendor. That was the poison. A fierce, exultant, destroying courage that sprang from an incurable nihilism of the soul. And it led him, not to triumph but to the very abyss. He had the courage to contemplate and obey the horror in his heart, to let it lead him wherever it would, to accept everything, to shrink from nothing, to make his choice deliberately and coldly, to feel the nearness of brutality like the touch of a hand, to enter the peculiar darkness that he knew awaited him and to be finally devoured by the abominable fancies of his soul. The true hero of our time; the modern Theseus, so to speak, who in an agony of realism casts away the thread in the middle of the labyrinth (248-49).

As for Samuel, he sees his own role as the opposite of Speght's —the search for a hero, hence for faith. That the hero turns out to be a "chimera" is, he decides, of no importance. "But the continual struggle, the continual defeat, the awareness of sin, the need of God—these are the things that have given man his own pathetic glory" (249).

At the end of the novel Leonard Speght is found, a corpse reduced by the powerful X ray of Africa to the pure geometry of his skeletal meaning. His corpse, in the posture of crucifixion, lies impaled on a rock a bit below the summit of Mount Nagalla.

Because of the preponderance of the word "darkness" in *Storm and Echo*, the reader is unable to resist the temptation to compare Speght with Joseph Conrad's Kurtz in *The Heart of Darkness*, the idealistically heroic European whom Africa malverses into a Satanic hero, a tribal God. Nor is there any reason to suppose that Frederic Prokosch is unaware of the parallel. His own admiration of Conrad[1] rules out the possibility that he would be unfamiliar with Conrad's best-known story. And so one must assume that the similarity offers deliberate homage to Conrad.

It is less clear as to how purposively Prokosch intends Mount Nagalla to recall the mountain of God in Ernest Hemingway's "The Snows of Kilimanjaro." Like the leopard or Hemingway's hero, Leonard Speght is found short of the summit. Once again, however, one can hardly believe that Prokosch would be oblivious to the parallel, and perhaps one can timidly postulate that Prokosch's aim is to bring to mind Conrad's and Hemingway's powerful stories, both of which are concerned with salvation and damnation, and to move through allusion to a somewhat similar thematic position. Mount Nagalla is beyond doubt the mountain of God in Prokosch's novel. More than Leonard Speght, the mountain is the symbolic destination of *Storm and Echo*. If it is held in awe and fear by the natives, the mountain draws the Europeans. Once, owing to a peculiar atmospheric chance, Samuel sees it briefly from afar, then it disappears. Later, when he is quite close, it assumes various aspects. At one time it looks merely ordinary; upon another occasion, it assumes the power and beauty of God, bringing harmony and a feeling of renewal.

When Joshua asks what the mountain means, the reactions of the white men are dissimilar but passionate. To Alessandro, it means the things he knows he will never find: love, fulfillment, and power. To Samuel, the mountain "means the inner darkness, the uncontrollable. Call it nature if you wish. Or call it instinct. Call it unreason. Call it evil. Call it the devil. I long to see it face to face. I long to recognize it and touch it. And finally free myself of it" (202). For Joshua, the mountain represents God. And, for Marius, it means death.

Like Conrad's Kurtz, Leonard Speght is destroyed by the irrational darkness at the center of the soul. Like Hemingway's Harry, Leonard Speght wishes to approach God; but he is denied

a complete salvation, though to both, admiration, like a consolation prize, is awarded for the struggle. However, Prokosch
grants both triumph and salvation to his narrator Samuel. For
his recognition of the powerful darkness within the nature of
life itself does ultimately free him from the darkness. He learns
that humanity possesses a pathetic yet noble continuity. He finds
it anchored in prehistory, staring through centuries of bestiality.
Somehow humanity survives, "indeciferable but electrifying"
(179).

Furthermore, Samuel sees the brilliant dance of butterflies
as an "exquisite" but "brainless joy" (228). Their harmless joy is
distinct from human aspiration. Nature itself is seen as an "inter-
minable anarchy" (175), whose confused dazzle creates a fear
which, in turn, creates a need for order and faith in something
beyond nature. In effect, then, Samuel's salvation is that of
"striking through the mask" of brainless nature, not of sinking
into the unconscious depths of atavistic emotion. The other
civilized men fail, but for Samuel: "The death wish was gone, the
will to live rose irresistibly, radiating from every leaf, every
breath of mountain air" (266).

When one considers that at the heart of Prokosch's feeling
about Europe in *The Asiatics* stands the conviction that society
is dying and furthermore wishes to die, Samuel's victory over
the death wish is significant. Still, because he is a civilized man,
he can never find the true beginnings of life, the foetal origin, the
real Africa of being. Yet Samuel carries within himself a recurring vision of childlike integrity, which preserves him from
despair. He does not cling in a neurotic conflict of perverse love
and sadistic tyranny to the black man as does one of the agents
for an export company. Neither tyrant nor lover, Samuel glimpses
in a supernatural trance the gray men, larger than ordinary men,
who symbolize an integration of the dark, primitive incipience of
human life with the ultimate evolution of civilized life.

Storm and Echo lacks the pristine charm of *The Asiatics*. It is
troubled by an unnecessary obscurity derived from Prokosch's
use of Africa on one occasion as a contrast to the civilized world
and on another occasion as a mirror image of civilization. One
village may evoke the heroic images of man's past; another,
withering in self-contemplation and homosexuality, quite the

opposite images. Nevertheless, despite the somewhat sullen and ambivalent surface, one is cognizant of a specific symbology in *Storm and Echo*. If this book is less engaging than *The Asiatics,* it is more aesthetically satisfying and mature. Yet *Storm and Echo* is less satisfying than the next in line of the travel novels which, while among the best of Prokosch's works, remains among the least known.

III Nine Days to Mukalla

Nine Days to Mukalla (1953), dedicated to the memory of George Santayana, opens with a plane crash on an island off the coast of Oman in the region of Ras Fartak. The pilot and one passenger are killed. The four survivors include two English women, the elderly Miss Todd, and Sylvia Howard, young but not pretty. They both have lived for a time in India and are returning to England. The other two survivors, Americans, are Dr. Moss, an archeologist who had been traveling in Persia, and David Gilbert, whose background is mysterious but who appears to be in the diplomatic service. The journey to Mukalla, from where the party will be able to take a boat to Aden, involves boat trips to other islands and to the city of Kumra, thence by caravan to Bir Ali, and finally to Mukalla. On the way Miss Todd dies of what appears to be a heart attack, Dr. Moss is murdered, and Sylvia Howard dies of exhaustion. Of the two Bedouins who steadfastly accompany the party, Idris dies of an infected bullet wound. David Gilbert and Ahmed survive, just as in *Storm and Echo* only Samuel and one native reach Mount Nagalla. There are other similarities between the two books.

Though Mukalla is not surrounded by the nimbus that deifies Mount Nagalla, the city remains always a point of mystery and urgency. When the party sets out, it is told that it will take nine days to reach Mukalla. Much later it is once again told the same thing; and, like the mountain, the city becomes the focal point of hope and despair. Arabia, whether sea, city, or desert, affects the characters much as Africa affects the Europeans in *Storm and Echo*. Early in the novel David feels "some antique horror prowling across the face of the world" (13). And midpoint in the novel, the mysterious Hirsch, a European who has become a Moslem, tells Dr. Moss that "Arabia . . . is like an X ray. It reveals the skeleton of humanity. Man is still a savage animal. And savage he will remain . . . for another million years" (98-99). One remembers that the X ray and the skeleton effect precisely the same metaphor deployed importantly in *Storm and Echo*.

The effect of the X ray is one—to employ the ambivalent term used by Prokosch in the novel—of revealing "wickedness" in the characters. Early in *Nine Days to Mukalla* Miss Todd, who is ill, asks if it is not well for wickedness "to come out into the open? As it does in Arabia"? (65). Late in the novel Sylvia observes that all of them have "become so wicked" that they have "turned into savages"! (202). The term is not synonymous with "evil." On the contrary, some of the wickedness appears to be merely the dissolution of a surface pretense or puritanism to which it is possible to say "good riddance."

Nine Days to Mukalla does not develop from a single point of view as do the other two journey novels; it moves by following the separate sensibilities of the different characters. In this respect it resembles *The Seven Who Fled* and *The Seven Sisters*. Nevertheless, the primary concern is the journey; and one is, furthermore, aware that David is the most important character. One guesses that he will survive, and the reader who has read others of the novels will recognize that the self-effacing, rather masked hero is cognate with the other heroes who fail in almost everything except their humanity. In so far as the momentum of the journey directs the action while the exotic and alien geography becomes a commentary on the civilized consciousness, *Nine Days to Mukalla* resembles the journey novels. "Only wandering," one of the Bedouins tells us, "is real. . . . To stay in one place becomes unreal. One forgets what the world is really like" (175).

Even the Bedouins, or at least most of them, are extrusions of the landscape rather than characters. Their virtues are those of a naïve nobility, a sinister innocence. Their vices are only corollaries of their virtues. If they are, for example, murderers, they are so as a corollary of their belief in fighting their enemies bravely, or in abiding by Islamic law. Certain niceties of sexual behavior are trivial to them because it is sexuality itself rather than the method of expression which is important. Only young Idris shapes up finally as a valid character. Impudent, charming, and lovable, he is "always gay, always smiling, hoping for fresh calamities" (52).

The Europeans and Americans are quite another matter, for it is through their complexities, their fears, and their hopes that meaning rises in the novel. Of greater import, it is through the contrast with one another that the novel obtains ultimately an allegorical structure. The primary contrast concerns Miss Todd and Dr. Moss.

Miss Todd, though she dies early in the book, remains a force throughout. She possesses a tolerance, sympathy, and staunchness not often found in Prokosch's characters. She, before any of the others, feels the influence of the Arabian wilderness in moments of great euphoria followed by moments of illness which adumbrate her death. Through Miss Todd, Prokosch rather slyly presents a microcosm of a subsidiary purpose of his novel. When asked by the Bedouins to recite a poem, she remains silent but remembers in her mind the following lines:

> Here at the fountain's sliding foot
> Or at some fruit-tree's mossy root,
> Casting the body's vest aside,
> My soul into the boughs does glide . . .

Prokosch does not identify the lines, but they come from Andrew Marvell's "The Garden." The poem both playfully and seriously involves the myth of the Garden of Eden in which Adam and Eve knew no shame, no self-consciousness. Shortly after thinking of the poem, Miss Todd observes that Ahmed keeps a poisonous snake in his shirt. He says that it is his *personal* snake and has bitten him three times. The first time he almost died, the second time he was very ill, but the third time he was only upset for an hour or two. When Miss Todd says that she would think he would dislike the snake, Ahmed smiles, replying that they are friends and have "forgiven each other" (25-26). The reader remembers that egotism is known as a "bosom serpent" in Spenser's *The Faerie Queene* as well as in Hawthorne's story "Egotism, or the Bosom Serpent." Neither Ahmed nor Miss Todd inhabits a garden exempt from egotism, but Ahmed has come to terms with himself. He will die, but not from a bite administered by a suppressed ego or self. In fact, Ahmed's snake has been tamed by being known. It peers at him with a wan, tired look.

Miss Todd herself is not endangered by a secret self, but she clairvoyantly perceives the secret selves in other characters. In particular she is cognizant of homely Sylvia's need for love; and, knowing that this need will surface, she asks David to be kind to her. Her perception leads always to kindly action. She gives David her jewels which, as it turns out, are the means of his getting to Mukalla. Her self-knowledge and the knowledge of others give her courage. Long after her death Idris speaks of her as a good spirit which has protected them. At the same time he speaks of Dr. Moss as an evil spirit who pursues them.

Dr. Moss, whether or not an evil spirit, does indeed contrast with Miss Todd. Though, like her, he feels a curious renewal in a wilderness which recalls but does not substantiate Eden, for him the renewal contains a sarcasm. Dr. Moss, who at forty-four has spent his mature life as an archeologist seeking out the dead artifacts of past history, finds himself in a region which history has by-passed. The result is that all his subdued passion for life in the present comes forth. And he is not immune to the bite of his buried life. When in a moment of exuberance he leaps on the shore, his heel is cut (quite as the heel of man must be bit by the serpent) by a sharp piece of obsidian. One ironically supposes that the obsidian is part of an arrowhead, an artifact, then; but it is one which, unlike a stone inscription, is a vestige of human passion. Later in the desert, just before his death, he finds another such chip of flint which he presses to his mouth, and it, too, brings blood.

The symbol of the obsidian chip is paralleled by Dr. Moss's behavior. In an episode both distressing and amusing, Idris, puzzled by the professor's interest in the past, offers to obtain for him a pretty girl or boy, possibly himself, modestly adding, "I am too old for you, I suppose? (31). Dr. Moss stalks away, but the reader knows that he has been tempted even more than he has been outraged. Later in Bir Barnut he comatosely follows a young Arab who has offered a dubious assignation. Recoiling, however, from the boy, he finds himself with a female prostitute whose ministrations make him feel "in touch with humanity as never before" (111). At the same times he feels a terrible fear.

He is unable after all to face himself. He feels safe only with the historical past. Because of his division and cowardice, the Arabs are frightened of him, thinking him a witch. In terror of the Arabs he treacherously steals some of Miss Todd's jewels from David and makes a bargain on his own to join a caravan to Mukalla. With compensatory treachery he is murdered in the desert, yet not before his suppressed passions, compressed to violence at last, come finally to the fore: Before he is murdered, he murders. Because, then, of a self-deception too long nurtured, he is isolated from humanity. The same self-deception leads him to terror and thence to death. He is truly a witch in the sense that he has worshiped a surrogate self, a false spirit.

Dr. Moss's fear of his real self is a fear of the animal portion of his being which he sees in a dream-vision as a "half-human silhouette, like a gorilla's" (34). He is not alone in his fear; Sylvia Howard also dreams of a gorilla, or at least of a gorilla's hand stretching from a minister's sleeve (43). And, like Dr. Moss, her latent sensuality stirs under the influence of the Arabian waste lands. But, unlike Moss, she has no complexity; she has signed no contract with the past. But then neither has she struck up a bargain with the future. Though she is no witch, she is scarcely like Miss Todd. She has little strength, little courage, little imagination. Because the hand of the gorilla, seen in her dream, stretches from the minister's sleeve, one surmises that her father, who had recently died in India, was a clergyman. Whether or not the surmise is right, everything about her hints of puritanical self-censorship. This censorship dissolves, and eventually she asks David to make love to her. She dies neither with the selfless courage of Miss Todd nor in the horror of the self-discovery of Dr. Moss, but of exhaustion in Mukalla. In one sense, she can only die when her false, imposed personality dies. In an extended sense, puritanism cannot survive the X rays of a savage land. For a bit the reader may feel a disappointment about the thinness of her characterization, the seeming pointlessness. But he will then see that just as Miss Todd and Dr. Moss contrast to produce an insight, so also do Sylvia Howard and David Gilbert.

David Gilbert is one of the most ambiguous of Frederic Prokosch's heroes, yet from a curious, narrow-angle of illumination within his ambiguity, he is finally the most believable, the

most interesting, and even the most clear. Near the beginning of
the novel he puzzles the good Miss Todd. She finds him "childlike" on the surface but "elusive underneath." She finds him
"beautiful" with his "youthful face" which is nevertheless deeply
lined. Simultaneously, she finds him "somehow cold, incomplete."
She thinks he is not quite a "typical American" (64-65).

These traits alter only slightly during the course of the novel.
Ahmed, who concludes that the American smiles to hide his
loneliness, asks him why he is "afraid of love" (132-33). And
when Sylvia asks if he will ever fall in love, David replies that
he tries "to love everyone a little" (177). If he is not precisely
cold, he is remote. It may be that the reader will also sense something profoundly strange about him. For example, when at one
point the omens seem favorable for the safety of the party, he
feels "his natural leaning toward melancholy" give "way to a
speculative optimism." And then very shortly afterward a butterfly alights on his wrist. "David cupped his hand over the insect
and held it between his fingers. The wings were of a watered
azure. He ran his thumb over them lightly; it was powdered with
iridescent dust. Dreamily, one by one, he plucked the wings from
the body. The butterfly fell to the ground, wriggling helplessly,
like a golden worm" (102-3).

Is there, one asks, a relationship between his "optimism" and
his inhuman behavior? With greater bewilderment, one asks if
there is any relationship between the man who dreamily mutilates an insect and who dreams like a poet of his past in America:

His mind reached back through the convolutions of India,
the shadowy gullies of Japan. It crossed the Pacific and rambled
over the great Wyoming hills; it wandered eastward and finally
came to rest on the shore of a river, where the birches shone
through the clear cool glow of a summer evening. Black-eyed
susans speckled the fields; sumac flowed over the hills. A dusty
path led up past the cornfield, which swayed lazily in the ruddy
air, rosy tassels dangling like manes through the crisp, fluted
ears. There was a barbed-wire fence along the edge of the
orchard. Hornets buzzed over the rotting crab apples; grasses
stirred over a passing snake. Dragonflies bright as mica went
zooming down to the banks, where the cattails bristled in the soft
gray mud. A family of turtles lay dozing on a trunk that floated

by. Not a sound, except for the humming of insects, and the far-off call of a whip-poor-will. Dusk gathered, the air grew filmy. And suddenly from the western hills rose the whistle of the freight train on its way to Prairie du Chien. Then stillness again; the sweet, harsh stillness of the inarticulate. Leaves came drifting down from the birches, bright as goldenrod, and tufts of thistledown lay floating in the windless air. This was the past which had shaped him; this was the intensity which lay buried in him. As his mind reached into the darkness, trying to grasp the nature of his loneliness, to touch the roots of that shapeless anxiety which never left him, what he saw was the vast, haunting savagery of an entire land—a land where desire hung like an aura in the very smell of the woods, where it fell and withered like the little crab apples in the grass. Was this the specter which haunted him? This perpetual yearning of a land that had grown too fast and had flung the mantle of power over a raw, barbarous body? (202-3).

There is a kinship between the mutilator of butterflies and the poet of nature, but it is one which is understood best in relationship with *The Asiatics* and with *Storm and Echo*.

The heroes of the two earlier journey novels have a personal aim in their journeys. For the young man in *The Asiatics,* it is happiness. For Samuel in *Storm and Echo,* the aim is to find the animal origin which, being found, may be triumphed over. For both, the realization of their aim is celebrated in a form of baptism. The hero of *The Asiatics* dives into a crystalline pool. Samuel sinks into the oozy, muttering waters of a primeval swamp, and this baptism is the beginning of his conquering the death wish and of his acceptance of his destiny as a civilized man to go on to whatever end history holds in store.

David Gilbert of *Nine Days to Mukalla* undergoes no such baptism. He has no need, for he carries within him the knowledge of the two earlier heroes. For he is, of course, the same hero. He possesses the same droll old-youthfulness of the boy in *The Asiatics,* who has a patch of white hair. He possesses the same tolerance of the strange world, the same hope for the future. At the same time he preserves some secret experience, hidden from all, even the reader. At times in the novel he seems on the verge of revealing the experience. The reader, however, if he does not know the secret, nevertheless knows the result of it. David Gilbert has made not peace but a working truce with himself in the way that Samuel has. Like Samuel who sees through the brainless joy of the butterflies, David can both admire the beauty and motion of nature and still see it coldly as mere phenomena, irrelevant in the last analysis to civilized man who has tragically broken free of nature. Hence for him no dream of a gorilla, no self-destroying sensuality stirs up from Arabia. Dr. Moss's life and Sylvia Howard's life in different ways are buried in and by the past; David's life is concerned with a future.

One returns at this point to Miss Todd's observation that David Gilbert is not quite a typical American. She is right. He is not the typical American of the past. But in his cool acquiescence in the mores of Bedouin and Britisher alike, his reserve and irony, and his ability to love everyone a little, he is not a bad ideal for the American of the future. Nor is his anxiety for himself and for his country a flaw. It is a burden, but it is the inevitable burden of the civilized man. It is better than the white man's burden, and it is also truer than the burden of the bliss and misery of animality.

We may profitably contrast the kind of American that David Gilbert is with another type in Prokosch's story, "The Murderer." A young American woman journalist, Miss Addison voices while in Portugal a post-war American view which amounts to a desire to convert all countries into replicas of America. She is idealistic; she believes in "health" and "freedom"; she is a walking Marshall Plan. One sees Prokosch's allegorical intent when a young Castilian who has been a political murderer makes love to her. This fiery young lover, this murderer, this intense "politician" becomes frightened to death of her. They both know suddenly that it is he who is weak and she who is strong.[2] She represents in other words, an American that would make the world over in her own image.

Having allowed a contrast which seems to be an accessory to political motive, one ponders finally the abstract configuration of *Nine Days to Mukalla*. The novel presents two English women and two American men. Can we take Miss Todd as a symbolic representation of the dying British Empire—firm, intelligent but now too old to endure? May we take Sylvia as a representation of an England rendered impotent by World War II? May Dr. Moss, with his dedication to the past, be seen as a now defunct, puritanical, and isolationist America? If so, then David Gilbert represents what would, of course, please Prokosch deeply: an international America.

CHAPTER 4

The Decadents

I The Skies of Europe

THE LONGEST and most intricately layered of Frederic Prokosch's novels, *The Skies of Europe*, was published in the year that America entered World War II. As it ponders the rise of Nazism, the Spanish Civil War, the aimless neurosis of France in the middle 1930's, the novel documents the social disorders of the time. To this day *The Skies of Europe*—along with such books as John Gunther's *Inside Europe* (1936), Edmund Wilson's *To the Finland Station* (1940), and Ernest Hemingway's *For Whom the Bell Tolls* (1940)—remains a vivid, valid portrait of Europe seen as a sleepwalker approaching an abyss. Yet it has purposes other than documentation: *The Skies of Europe* is also a love story, and, in its deepest commitment, a story about the artistic life.

The novel opens in Paris in 1936. The first person narrator, Philip, a young American journalist, frequents cafes where intellectuals and aesthetes discuss Marxism and fascism in an atmosphere of spiritual drought and cultural collapse. He falls in with the Russian expatriate painter Alexis and his Ruthenian mistress Saskia with whom he himself becomes infatuated. The scene shifts abruptly with Philip's going to Munich where he visits Frau Meyer and her family at the Pension Lucrezia where he had stayed as a student thirteen years before. He finds that the rise of Hitlerism has altered the family. Those whom he had once known and loved as individuals now speak in a "litany" of self-pity and justification for the "new Germany." The implications of change come to a crisis in the violent quarrel between Frau Meyer's sons. Dietrich has become a Nazi; Stefan has not.

Philip then moves on to Austria where as a child he had lived with his Uncle Alois who keeps an inn in a village near Salzburg. This section of the novel serves as an idyllic contrast with the complications of Paris and the chilling simplifications of Munich. True, intimations of change drift in like smoke from a distant fire; but, in general, this first Austrian episode shows a Europe of the old standards of goodness and honesty. The old but vigorous Uncle Alois in particular, with his love of work, his liveliness and intelligence, embodies the ideals of a Europe of the past. Here Philip has an affair, full-bodied but rather half-hearted, with a peasant girl, Maria, whose freshness and spontaneity contrast with the rather sinister energies of Saskia.

Yet it is Saskia who draws him, against his better judgment, back to Paris. In the meantime, Saskia and Alexis have quarreled, and she has given up painting in favor of dancing. Philip for a short time becomes her lover, though she does not love him. The affair progresses in the painful cadences of Catullus' *odi et amo* until Stefan Meyer, disgusted with Germany, comes to Paris. Stefan and Saskia fall so ecstatically in love with each other that they are oblivious to all else.

Philip goes to Barcelona and retreats with a band of Loyalists before Franco's advance. The impressions of the Civil War are of aesthetic rather than political interest. Philip wanders, somewhat like Don Quixote, across the fiercely beautiful land where war seems—as it does in some of Stephen Spender's poems about the Spanish Civil War—a strange irrelevancy. As the Loyalists continue to fall back, Philip makes his way to the French border and, after a comic interlude in southern France, returns again to Paris.

Saskia's and Stefan's love has not diminished. Indeed it is such a "violent mutual passion" as to be "abnormal" (360). Their incredible constancy—not their love—has a profound effect on Saskia's former lover, Alexis. In a storm during a picnic he murders Stefan, arranging for the deed to appear an accident. Though Saskia and Philip know that Alexis is a murderer, they do not tell.

The tragedy of Stefan's death sends Philip wandering again— again to Munich, again to Austria. In both places the pace of change has accelerated. His childhood friend Dietrich has become more frail physically as he has increased his dedication to

the Nazi philosophy of "strength." In Austria the death of his
Uncle Alois symbolizes the death of the noble past. The novel
stretches into a coda of wandering—a searching, really, for the
city of humanity; and it finishes in a reunion with Saskia.
"Nothing," he vows, "would ever take her away again. Through
fire and snow I'd follow her, through sickness and hunger, through city after city" (500). Considering Saskia's
promiscuity, her moral worthlessness, her pretense, one wonders
why Philip should dedicate himself to her. The reason cannot
be any more simple than Saskia herself is, and she is intricate.

Saskia is only one representation of a number of Prokosch's
heroines who do not love the hero and who somewhat obsessively drift from one bed to another. These heroines, like
Lydia in *The Idols of the Cave* or Irina in *The Conspirators,* are
often Slavic by descent. At moments of intensity the hero sees
"Mongolian planes" in their faces. They are apt to have a mole,
like a beauty mark, as does the little heroine in *Night of the
Poor.* (Saskia's mole, unfortunately, shifts from a position at the
left of the nose in the beginning of the novel to a more prominent
position on the nose itself later on.) These incidental similarities
among the heroines of those novels which strive to be more or
less realistic suggest, of course, that Prokosch works through
some kind of feminine archetype. We cannot discover the reason
for his choice, of course. But a far more important fact about
these heroines than that of their similarities or their origin is
their tendencies to be artists of one sort or another. They dance,
sing, or dabble at painting. They are, however, never fully
successful in these aesthetic pursuits. But, if they fail as artists,
they possess great power. Theirs is an animal power which they
understand and appreciate superlatively and use with feline
subtlety. Though they do not ever really love the exasperated
hero, they are always immensely pleased and smiling when they
bring him to a pitch of physical excitement.

In only one instance does their promiscuity lead to pregnancy,
and then a simple abortion restores this heroine to her original
state quite unchanged. And "unchanged" is an appropriate word,
for, though the heroine grows older and sometimes ages alarm-
ingly, she does not in any psychological or spiritual sense change.
These fatal women are, we are told, the only really innocent

creatures in the world; for they believe they are innocent. They are the true virgins of time and space.

These heroines, though doubtless based upon one or more persons whom Prokosch has observed, obviously embody some human truth, as Prokosch sees it, in their persons and their actions. Saskia is—both despite and because of her animality, her promiscuity, her frailty and beauty—an incarnation of an aspect of humanity itself. Surely it is for that reason that Philip will follow her from city to city.

The nearly hopeless love, as hopeless as the love of humanity, is outlined by symbol. The most telling symbols are those of a toy horse, an old man's story, and a statue of Mercury. Saskia gives Philip the horse rather casually when he is leaving the first time for Munich. As it is raining outside, he carries it home under his coat. He turns the key to its mechanism and feels the horse prance against his ribs, like a heart. Later in his room, he watches it go through its staccato movements. It looks at him "imploringly." Its paint is sticky with the rain (43). The image of the horse ramifies, of course. It reminds the reader of Saskia, herself, of her relentless dance of life. It reminds him, too, of Philip's own fatal relationship to that dance. The wet, sticky paint possesses the *feel* of fallibility, the coursing of heartbreak.

The grotesque old man appears twice. The first time, Philip has just become aware of "the merest shadow of degradation" in Saskia. The old man comes by in the street singing a song about a little sailor who had never put to sea. Less like a little sailor than the ancient mariner, he tells Saskia and Philip his story. Long ago he had married a girl named Sophonisbe as "white and gentle as a lamb."

> And what do you suppose? A week after the wedding I came home and found her in bed with a stranger! . . . So I picked up the *pot de chambre* and broke it over his head. That seemed only reasonable, under the circumstances. And that was the end of him. It developed, unpleasantly enough, that I'd broken his skull. Right in two, like a Brazil nut. They threw me into jail for a week or two, merely out of courtesy. And as for my lovely Sophonisbe, I never saw her again: she vanished into thin air. And I've been looking for her ever since . . . in Brest, Rouen, Nantes, even down as far as Poitiers (162-63) . . .

The parallel between Philip's love for Saskia and the old man's love for Sophonisbe is clear. And it is made brutally clear by the farcical quality of the story and by the mawkishness of the old man himself. One sees, also, a premonition of the ending of the novel in the old man's search for his love from city to city. When Philip encounters Sophonisbe's husband again, he already knows the story, and he has in his own way now experienced it for himself. And so to the old man's consternation and annoyance, he anticipates with bitterness the turnings of the squalid little drama (214).

The most elaborate of the symbolic images is that of a statue of Mercury which stands in a small garden below the apartment shared by Alexis and Saskia. Broken and eroded, the statue's impotence and lifelessness are mentioned at several points early in the novel. On an evening shortly before the fatal picnic where Stefan is murdered, Philip and Alexis from the apartment window watch as Saskia dances in the garden while Stefan plays his violin: "As she danced, the white naked statue of Mercury with little wings on his feet grew alive: his loins glowed like ripe fruit. It was he, the fleet-footed one, who seemed to be distilling the magical hunger and delight" (359).

The toy horse and the old man are sad omens for Philip. The statue of Mercury is even sadder, for Philip will never so perfect his love with Saskia that together they will bring life to a weather-beaten statue. Yet, his inability to achieve a violent mutual passion must ultimately be seen to be not merely less than catastrophic but even salvational. For such a passion contains the germs of its own self-destruction. It is a passion that, in becoming as impersonal as great art, has also become inhuman. Such perfection may inspire Alexis to murder, but in all truth the death has already taken place. When the statue of Mercury glows with life, the lovers have conversely become as stylized as the statue was. If one remembers what happens to human lovers who aspire to be immortal in Yeats's early poems or in Keats's *"La Belle Dame sans Merci"* he knows what cosmic revenge awaits them. To fall short, then, as does Philip, of such consummation is to remain human, to save one's life. One may ironically add that Stefan's murder saves Saskia's life. As engaging as Prokosch's philosophy of love is, it is only one of three

lines which by intersecting make a configuration. The other two
lines involve, as indicated earlier, art and politics.

Artists of one sort or another crowd a number of Prokosch's
novels. Almost always Prokosch takes a rather amused view of
his dancers, painters, and writers. He is fond of having them
attribute preposterous titles to pictures or to poems. These
moments of sarcastic parody in part reveal his awareness of the
high degree of fraudulence in all art, whether good or bad;
in part they reveal his awareness of the overpowering probability that the artist will fail.

In *The Skies of Europe* Saskia fiddles with the "pointillisme"
style of painting. Despite her absurd earnestness, she suddenly
abandons painting for dancing. One never supposes that she
possesses much talent and one wonders why she craves to be some
kind of creator. It is a different matter with Alexis. Behind his
wearisome barrier of boring talk stirs a creative energy. Something akin to tragedy accompanies his desperate changes of
style. Much more is at stake for him than for Saskia, and his
failure, all the greater that he comes closer than Saskia to success,
corrodes his soul, inflicting a fatal imbalance which at length con-
tributes to his manic murder of Stefan. In Saskia and Alexis,
the theme of the artist is accessory to the theme of love.

But other characters serve better to clarify the plight of the
artist as Prokosch sees it. At the very beginning of *The Skies of
Europe*, Philip meets three writers who reappear from time to
time. These are Adolphe Wintherberger; Hercule Lapeyrade,
a Marxist poet with an "unshakable faith in 'progress,' in 'revolt,'
in 'historical necessity'"; and Hippolyte Barbezieux, an *avant-
garde* poet, an aesthete with no faith at all in the future (4, 6).
Although Prokosch cartoons these characters, he does so merci-
fully, treating them with tolerance and affection. What he smiles
at is their want of an individual view; what he sympathizes with
is their failure as artists.

Wintherberger is an incredible old bore. He has lived on
his memory of having known Mallarmé in the heyday of *sym-
bolisme*. Literary fashion has long since passed him by, and,
aiming at perfection, he has written almost nothing. Ironically,
while he has aimed at a perfection "like Flaubert" and pre-
ferred the "classical fatigues" of Mallarmé to the "clay" of

Baudelaire, he has secretly consoled himself by collecting pornography. His wasted life cannot be salvaged; he deserves ridicule, but Philip, aware of what it means to fail as a poet, greets him with flattering kindness. He says, "You are Adolphe Wintherberger, the distinguished poet, I believe?" The kindness has its touching reward: "The shimmer of childish expectation in his mottled face was transformed into a brief, mild glow of ecstasy. In that small dark garden behind the cathedral he had actually discovered, at this very moment, a tiny trace of something which had eluded him for years, for decades: just a whiff of prestige, a hint of celebrity" (340-41).

Lapeyrade and Barbezieux are not frozen in the past; they are stuck in the present; but their failure is as certain as Wintherberger's. Wintherberger dies unaltered, fading back into the time which produced him. The failure of Lapeyrade and Barbezieux appear in their significant alterations of person: A bit beyond the midpoint of the novel Philip runs into them after not seeing them for some time:

> Lapeyrade had grown thinner and sharper. He had become a type: the aesthetic puritan. There were metallic gray streaks on his temples. His eyes were still clear and serene but there was a touch of bitterness, of defiance in them now. His ascetic profile had turned into a hatchet face. Below the surface of his voice could be heard a low crackling and hissing, like a grindstone sharpening the edge of his words.
>
> As for Barbezieux, he had taken on a bit of weight, his chin was heavier and squarer: his hair was thinner, scarcer, wearier. The sly, stubborn Gascon peered more distinctly through his little pink eyes. He had a new and rather ponderous way of rubbing his chin and raising his brows. Yes, he looked a bit smug; a bit oily even (334).

It is noteworthy that at this time both have given up writing poems. And to see that the aesthetic puritan and the smug bourgeois indicate the extreme possibilities of the artist's failure is to apprehend one of the most important aspects of Prokosch's whole view of life.

The theme of the artist *manqué* affects the theme of love, driving the ambitious but talentless Saskia into wanton restiveness and urging the talented, but not great, Alexis to violence. The theme enters also into the novel's concern with political history. The most dramatic presentation of the rise of Nazism involves the quarrel in Munich between the two brothers, Stefan and Dietrich. The allegory is not at all arcane. Dietrich has been a sickly child, but as a youth he disciplines his body and grows surprisingly muscular. When he becomes a full-fledged Nazi, however, he "relapses," grows frail again, as if Hitlerism were a kind of spiritual childhood disease. In this respect he resembles the Nazi Hugo Wildenbruch in *The Seven Who Fled*, who beneath his Wagnerian romantic armor is dying of the tuberculosis which had deprived him of his mother.

At a more revealing, as well as more subtle allegorical level, the character of the artist, Onkel Willi, broadens the reader's impression of the malaise of Nazi Germany. As a poor, unsuccessful artist in Munich he had painted decadent subjects: perverts, pimps, and the like. During Philip's final visit to Munich, he has become "successful." He paints:

> Nordic gods and goddesses, naked, brown, muscular, all engaged in actions both useful and wholesome—tilling fields, nursing the young, feeding pigs, waving flags. . . .
> Perhaps some of the old gusto had gone; after all, those old degenerates of his had a certain intensity and zest about them, even a quaint charm. These new figures were stony, stalwart, sexless.
> Yet, if one looked closely, there was a curious similarity: in the lack of humor, in the slightly morbid exaggeration. Where his creatures before had a shrunken miasmic pallor about them, now they were bulbous with muscles, luridly red-cheeked. Their resemblance to mankind was equally remote and only slightly less alarming. The sentimentality had moved in the opposite direction, that was all (423).

Like Barbezieux, Onkel Willi has gotten fat. Like him, he has also grown smug, spiritually lazy. But Onkel Willi is dangerous in a way that Barbezieux is not. Though he has failed in his high calling as an artist, he has become nevertheless successful in another way, so that his moral obtuseness is at the disposal of an insane politics.

One other artist appears in the novel. In a particularly impressive passage, a person, unnamed but obviously Hitler, comes to the tearoom where Philip is talking with Dietrich. Prokosch's portrait is illuminating:

> But what I found far more interesting, and even moving, was something else in the man. Absolute power hung over him like a stiff white shroud, and yet, in his shifting ink-blue eyes, in his bad teeth and pudgy hands even in the flakes of dandruff that clung to his hair, were visible the signs of an earlier life—the furtive and tireless intensity of the unsuccessful artist, the fanatical, heartless violence of the neglected poet: which now, in this atmosphere of cozy teapot and brocades, had softened and swollen into a wondrous, self-intoxicated bloom (395-96).

Now, *The Skies of Europe* is a story of love and of the drift of Europe toward war; why then does Prokosch worry these primary concerns with these portraits of unsuccessful artists, even reducing Hitler's neurosis to that of "the neglected poet"? Let the reason be stated first with simplicity. The urge to create in Prokosch's view is a basic urge in the human condition. The urge to create emancipates man from nature and tragically separates him from other forms of life. Between the boundaries or emancipation and tragic isolation, he must find his destiny; and, in so doing, commit himself to action, whether good or bad. The dangers of life, therefore, are the dangers of creation. These are the dangers of fanatical repression, diabolism—or of corpulent self-satisfaction. Behind the monstrous behavior of Alexis the murderer, and of Hitler, crouches the frustration of the artist who has never brought himself into fulfillment. Equally, behind the failures of all mankind stands man's own failure to shape his true existence, to create his soul. One observes, of course, that Prokosch considerably broadens the concept of an artist, making it into a large metaphor for society itself.

History, for Frederic Prokosch, contains as it does for T. S. Eliot, "cunning passageways," unpredictables. But in the long run "the only pertinent history of men is the history of man's soul" (276). In Spain, Philip learns that in the defeated, rather than in the victorious, the seeds of regeneration have been sown. Similarly, though he sees social decadence everywhere about him in Europe, he sees the phoenix nesting among the lowly and the abandoned. Thus, while Prokosch nostalgically laments the passing of an age—an end of the old Europe and of the decent civilization—he also senses that some vitality is dumbly stirring in the ashes. The true, irredeemable decadents, then, are those who self-righteously seek power for its own sake and who thus cease to believe in humanity. Such are the Nazis in *The Skies of Europe*. At a comic level, though still with seriousness, Prokosch tenders to the reader a character who is the very antipode of the self-torturing, self-enslaving fascist.

Ignace Pélissier, whom Philip meets in southern France on his return from Spain, is one of the few comic characters in Prokosch's novels. He is entirely a rogue. He has "stolen, counterfeited, seduced, blackmailed, swindled, burgled, embezzled and assaulted" (299). Prokosch can, however, find reason to admire Pélissier; and it is of interest that the terms of his admiration include the idea of his being an "artist."

> His very voice brought life, warmth, even truth: for he was above all, an artist. And like all real artists, detached from the bondages of society. But his art lay in action, not observation; in destruction, not creation; thus freeing him even from the bondages of art—the bitterness, the self-doubts, the self-torments. There was no such thing as failure in his style of career . . . He was the only man I'd ever known who had emerged triumphant over the illness of his age and setting. He was, in his way, a pure and perfect specimen. And in his way, he loved mankind (299-300).

The reader will object that the metaphor of the artist has been overextended. It does not really illuminate Hitler and Pélissier. Agreed, it does not. But it does indicate the intensity with which Prokosch regards the artist—an intensity further revealed in a later novel.

II A Ballad of Love

Although *A Ballad of Love* (1960) covers a longer span of time than *The Skies of Europe*, as well as an even greater geographical range, the two novels have much in common. They work with similar characters and problems. That *A Ballad of Love* came from the same lumber is strongly suggested by the fact that it duplicates a scene from the earlier novel.[1]

A Ballad of Love, told by first-person narrator Henry, opens with the child's early life in Austria. Upon the death of his father, a puppet-master, Henry stays for a time in the establishment of an effeminate baron. He is then sent to Texas to live with his Uncle Adelbert, a composer and violinist. Here he encounters Stella, his cousin, whom he is destined to love through the remainder of the novel. When Uncle Adelbert goes mad, Henry once more is displaced; this time he goes to Uncle Claudius and Aunt Elfrida in Wisconsin. Here he meets Tony Cavallero who is, after Stella, the most important character in Henry's story. After he and Tony have an accident in a stolen car, Henry is sent to his Aunt Ursula in Pennsylvania. He attends Llewellyn College, evidently modeled after Haverford, where he writes poems, plays tennis, and makes friendships of one sort or another. Henry, however, feels something sterile, even inhuman, about college life and leaves without graduating. With a small amount of money supplied by his Aunt Ursula, he goes for a time to New York and writes poetry. At length he sails for Paris.

The narration up to this point is only occasionally sharp in detail; much of it moves in a desultory fashion. One recognizes the intent, that of a prelude, a portrait of the artist as a young man; but Prokosch does not himself seem to care much about the early material, so that the novel presents an immense and not very useful front porch. It only really begins after Henry's arrival in Paris.

While living in Pennsylvania, Henry had briefly seen Stella and Tony again, and they both show up again in Paris. Each of these characters, Henry included, is a rogue-artist with comic as well as tragic facets. Stella, who has tried ballet, becomes a nightclub singer. Tony is a painter. Henry continues to write poems but he also poses for his sculptor friend Boris. With Boris' mistress, Maggy, he dances at a club called "The Box of Sardines." The dances are preposterous, pornographic frauds with titles such as "Etruscan Fertility Rite" and "Manchurian Harvest Dance," titles amusingly reminiscent of some concocted by Ted Shawn and José Limon. For a short time Henry also becomes a gigolo, the kept boy of a rather charming and fey harpy, a comtesse whose name, Isabelle de la Harpe, is less than subtle.

Stella is not a very successful singer; but, like Saskia, she desires success above everything else, as if it were power or happiness. In her search, she shifts her erotic arrangements without scruple, eventually taking up with Paolo, a millionaire. But she falls in love with Tony. Tony is not only more talented than Stella but more ruthless. Like Stella, he tends to seek power through his sexuality. For his part he takes up with a rather pathetic Jewess who, like Paolo, has money.

Together these characters form not an eternal triangle but a dying polygon in which Henry and Paolo love Stella who, like Melanie, loves Tony, who perhaps loves himself. As soon as this polygon comes into being, the characters begin to erode. The moderately comic fallen world of Stella and Tony turns into lurid depravity. For several reasons the characters are separated when Poland is invaded, but eventually they come together again in Tangiers. In North Africa, Tony rather casually murders Paolo and is himself as casually murdered by an Arab. The epilogue—set in time six years later in Paris, when the war is over—informs Henry and the reader that Stella died during the war in a Saharan village.

This summary, which grasshoppers over a good deal of the action, indicates that *A Ballad of Love* is a busy book. In most ways it is an indefensible failure. However, it does tend to define most clearly Prokosch's obsession with the defeated artist. In pursuing the problem, there is little reason to say much about Stella who, in her sexual force, her eagerness for success, and her preservation of an innocence despite her promiscuity, is only a hyperbolic Saskia. Tony Cavallero, on the other hand, offers an opportunity for additional insights.

In Prokosch's third novel *Night of the Poor* (1939), another Tony (Tony Gonzales), a Mexican boy, joins the young hero for a short while on his American safari. Like Tony Cavallero, the Mexican boy is knowing, experienced, and devil-may-care. These qualities attract the hero; nevertheless, he sees "in Tony with distrust something of himself: something of himself grown footloose and shady" (94). Such also is Henry's relationship with Tony Cavallero. For Tony, even as a boy in Wisconsin, carries within him the foreknowledge of his own self-destructive-ness. When Henry asks him what he will do when he grows up, Tony says he will sail around the world, shoot tigers, then return, and "buy a palace and marry a princess." Having said this, he draws a picture in the sand: "A bulging mosque at one end with a little minaret beside it . . . And in the corner he drew his own inscrutable symbol, like Whistler's butterfly: a sword with a two-headed serpent coiled around it." He says that he thinks such a place exists in Africa. It does, of course, for Tony is relentlessly drifting toward his death in Tangiers.

But if Tony is drifting toward his own death, he also is Henry's savior literally and figuratively. He saves Henry from drowning, but more profoundly he exemplifies a virile splendor that Henry loves and unconsciously chooses as a model for his own conduct later when he reacts against the sterility of college. Tony is an alter ego to Henry, even though he is, in most ways, his opposite. Like the alter ego in Conrad's "The Secret Sharer," Tony represents a self of violence and impulse, a self never quite to be surrendered to, and yet a self which has a beauty and a peculiar capacity to save others, though not itself. Such is Tony's symbolic as well as symbiotic relationship with Henry.

In Tony's own right as a character, those very aspects which give him value for Henry bring ruin to himself. A creature of animal impulse, his fatal flaw is that his animal instinct for self-preservation plays him false. The self-concern of a fox will not work for a human being who wants to be a great artist. Thus Henry senses under Tony's Caravaggio beauty, under the "dark, supple grace . . . a lingering whiff of criminality" (73). Nor is it merely that Tony heartlessly cadges money from Henry; nor even that he steals for the psychic thrill of stealing; not even that he murders. His ultimate sin emerges from his contempt for other human beings. He ironically believes that his art exempts rather than involves him in the life of the world. His exemption, how-ever, is different from Pélissier's freedom, for in no way is he able to love mankind. "Call me a rascal if you want to," he says to Henry. "I can't help it. I'm an artist. I'm heading for some-thing bigger and much more important than the rest of you" (289-90).

In these words one sees the true meaning of Tony. He has

become the artist who has committed the sin of pride. His Africa is the Africa of the French poet Arthur Rimbaud, who after all his inhuman ardor, his self-sacrifice and sacrifice of humanity for the sake of poetry, gave up writing before he was twenty and went to Africa to die a spiritual death long before his actual one. And Tony has, in all truth, never believed in anything outside his own immediate self. As a boy he tells Henry that he does not want after death to become a ghost or an angel; he wants merely to be dead (73).

Stella's death in the desert parallels Tony's. Henry says of them that "They were twins, of course, in a way. Decadent barbarians; *manqué* artists; beautiful and twisted adolescents" (294). Twelve hundred miles from Algiers, Stella dies, a nymphomaniac and a drug addict. Significantly, she has carried with her a volume of Rimbaud's poetry, "a memory of old times" (310).

III *The Artist in a Decadent World*

Prokosch's gallery of artists does not cheer the heart. They are old and passé; or young and desperate; or successful and corrupt; or, like Tony and Stella, they are the twisted adolescents, burning out in a quest for an illumination beyond their reach. Prokosch *is*, as a matter of fact, cheerless on this score. He wrote late in 1962:

> . . . writing as a career is full of grief: for the "successful" ones comes a cheapening, a vulgarization, a gradual (or swift) decline, a removal from the realms of true art; for the "unsuccessful" comes bitterness, sterility, or a kind of aesthetic puritanism. I was lucky to be neither, quite. Certainly never a "success," thank the Lord, and I *hope* not quite a failure. So that now I am well into post-maturity and feel free and dedicated to pure excellence. I shall never write as well as I'd like. But I have won my own secret, invisible triumph, (if you can grasp the meaning of these words!) [2]

One pauses to note that the phrase "aesthetic puritan" had been used twenty years earlier in *The Skies of Europe*. As to "the meaning of these words," that is a gambit to be avoided. But the words do inspire further insights.

Frederic Prokosch's obsession with the artist recalls similar obsessions in the twentieth century: those of James Joyce, William Butler Yeats, and others. In particular, Thomas Mann comes to mind. As is commonly known, Mann conceived of the artist as a kind of "criminal," outside and opposed to society. His picaresque hero, Felix Krull—who is not entirely different from Prokosch's rogue, Ignace Pélissier—is an allegorical representation of the criminal artist. At a more relevant level, the murky artist in Mann's incomparable story, "Mario and the Magician" exemplifies an artist whose "criminality" has gone too far. His natural egotism has become narcissism; his natural instinct for power has become fascism; his natural love of life has become, on the one hand, a lugubrious puritanism and, on the other, a whirlpool of corruption. True, Mann obviously offers Cipolla as a pervasive example of fascism; but, as has been little recognized, Cipolla also represents what happens to art in a world slipping into decadence and experimenting desperately in the monstrous laboratory of totalitarianism. And so it is, too, with the degradation of Prokosch's characters such as Tony Cavallero and Stella. If they fail as artists—or, to put it better, if they fail the world as artists—the world is partly at least to blame for their failure. Tony and Stella reflect the world, and the world reflects them. Their evil is the world's evil.

One other enlightening parallel suggests itself. In 1936 Stephen Spender published a collection of short stories, several of which strongly suggest that he had been deeply influenced by the views, if not by the methods, of Thomas Mann. Among these stories, "The Dead Island" deals with a young poet who is an alcoholic and a thief. Every life he touches is harmed. A friend attempts to explain him as follows:

> Now I have said—and indeed it seems gratefully obvious— that he is shut out from the surrounding world. . . . Yet another though terrible way of expressing this is to say that he *is* the world . . . In him is incarnated the moment when a civilization really begins to lose grip when . . . Art is hoarded away where it is least valuable, in the minds of artists who cannot express themselves . . .

> Where there is tyranny and fear, nothing is created. How,
> then, shall one condemn an artist who, being unable to create,
> lives in his own being, the poem, the dance, the madness,
> which he apprehends from the world around him?[3]

If one discounts the slightly hysterical left-wing cadences of
the young Spender, these words help to illuminate Prokosch's
decadent artists in a decadent world. Such an understanding is
necessary before one can comprehend Prokosch's notion of what
constitutes an artist who, unlike Tony, saves himself. This matter
brings us to a consideration of the narrators of *The Skies of
Europe* and of *A Ballad of Love*. They have much in common;
one is tempted to say that they have Prokosch in common.

Like the hero of *The Asiatics*, Philip and Henry, far from
being forceful characters, seem almost to lack substance. They
are in a western environment carrying out the injunction in
The Asiatics to remain "humble." Henry actually irritates Stella,
who calls him a chameleon without character of his own, for
he changes always in response to whomever he is with. One
notes that Prokosch not only prefers the chameleon as a symbol
for Henry, but that Henry is the only character who is saved
in *A Ballad of Love*. Nor is he saved because his behavior is
much nicer or more moral than Stella's and Tony's. He admits
that he, too, is a "degenerate scoundrel" (262-63). But whether
or not he is a scoundrel, one notes that he, unlike the others,
never uses people, never takes advantage of them, never destroys
them. Except for his behavior with the harpy countess, who
roundly merits the treatment, he acts out of love, a love which
is directed out rather than in, just as the chameleon shows what
is outside himself rather than what is within. Henry's relation
with people parallels his relation to art. He behaves humbly,
cooly, even amusedly toward his poetry. In fact, at the end of the
novel he no longer writes poetry, we are told; but he has become
a journalist—as was Philip in *The Skies of Europe*. The reader is
invited to translate "journalist" to "novelist." The point is that
Prokosch suggests that overweening ambition and impatient
overemphasis of success lead the artistic personality into the
winter forest of failure or into the ambush of success, or worse,
to Rimbaud's spiritual death in the desert.

But does not all this humility and self-husbandry seem feckless? It would—if it were all that Prokosch felt on the subject. It remains to observe, however, that his tragic categories of artists do not include the great artist, any more than the great artist is a character in his novels. But it is implicit that great art, if it should come at all, comes as a result of humility, restraint, and patience. There is no way of forcing it.

Reviewing in 1939 Yeats's *Last Poems and Two Plays*, Frederic Prokosch appropriately commented on the phenomenon of the fulfillment of an artist in his later years, and "the great freshening power that even old age might conceivably provide."[4] Later he repeated these observations in reference to Dame Edith Sitwell: "Miss Sitwell, like Yeats, stands as a shining and awe-inspiring example of how a poet, after a prolonged and some-times hesitant apprenticeship, can finally in old age acquire his true idiom, can strike, so to speak at the real core of his in-spiration at last, and can produce, even in the tragic and despair-ing meditation of old age, a passionate, resonant, triumphant justification of a long career."[5] The keyword is "apprenticeship." The word connotes work, modest self-effacement, and patience; it does not connote frenetic ambition or disaster. Perhaps if one could hope for such a late flowering, he could speak, as he nears the age of sixty, of having won his "own secret, invisible triumph."

CHAPTER 5

The Peripheries of War

I The Conspirators

ALL OF PROKOSCH'S WORK reveals an abiding sensitivity to omens of historical change. And while one hears, like Kubla Khan, "ancestral voices prophesying war" through much of his work, only three of his novels deal very specifically with World War II. These novels—*The Conspirators* (1943), *Age of Thunder* (1945) and *The Idols of the Cave* (1946)—are quite different from one another. *The Conspirators*, easily the most unified and tightly written of Prokosch's books, exploits a multiple viewpoint, somewhat in the manner of *The Seven Who Fled*. *Age of Thunder* follows the episodic formula of *The Asiatics*, but it does not regard geography in quite the same suggestive way. *The Idols of the Cave* is relatively realistic and conventional in purpose. It stays throughout with the same set of characters, and its structure depends on their inter-relationships. Different however, as these three novels are in method, they nonetheless have a common body of thematic material, and they inhabit the peripheries of the war. There are no battle scenes.

The Conspirators is set in Lisbon in the darkest hours of World War II. The beautiful city is filled with exiles from all the invaded and overturned countries. Among the exiles, of course, are spies and counterspies, the fascists and those who plot against fascism. The hero, Vincent Van der Lyn, is a Dutch exile, who is imprisoned, as the novel opens, for "political unreliability." He escapes from prison and in a period of less than twenty-four hours, discovers his betrayer, the Nazi agent Hugo von Mohr, who poses as an anti-fascist Anglophile, and kills him. The very simple movement of the novel is complicated only by the fact that Vincent's former lover and co-conspirator, Irina Petrova, has during his incarceration become von Mohr's mistress.

The action, while producing a conventional suspense rare in Prokosch's work, is of less importance than the atmosphere of haunting historical change or the various portraits which have great fidelity. One has good reason to suspect that a number of the incidental portraits are based upon actual refugees in Lisbon where Prokosch spent a year after the invasion of France. In an article written as a journalistic account of Lisbon during this time, Prokosch includes a maharajah much like the one who appears briefly in *The Conspirators,* and there are also other similarities.[1]

The exiles in the novel are two general sorts—those who being newly exiled or less "engaged" are motivated largely by intact ideals, and those who have long been engaged and are changed as a result. But for both types, the mystique of the conspirator has a profound effect. The whole of Chapter XXII is devoted to the conversation of a naïve Polish painter, a naïve Serbian poet, and a cosmopolitan Greek. Their talk ranges from political generalizations to art and love. But, when Van der Lyn passes near, in flight from pursuing police, they intuitively understand the situation. "The instincts of conspiracy," Prokosch observes of this situation, "are beyond the region of words; they are electrical and unerring" (214). The three exiles, who have seen Van der Lyn's flight, give no information to the police. They tremble with excited sympathy for the stranger whom they know only as a "conspirator." This chapter, which is beautifully done and which could easily stand as a short story in its own right, encourages the reader to generalize from the three characters and, like them, to see all the world as engaged in intrigue and treachery. And indeed such a generalization is just what Prokosch seeks throughout the novel to impose on his readers.

The professional conspirators intensify and focus the general atmosphere, but they are of peculiar interest, too, for the role of conspirator mutilates the personality. The mysterious Spaniard, Pedro Quintanilla, who directs Vincent toward his betrayer, has "fought for a vision of life, but with a tenacity and cunning that sprang not from an outer vision but an inner devastation" (56). He has lived a series of disguises until the disguise has grown more important than self. As a result, in a total violation of personality, he has become effeminate, fond of wearing rouge. Similarly, fascist Hugo von Mohr has become a mask of classically cold beauty. Von Mohr, however, represents more than a conspirator: he stands also as a model of fascism. A friend tells Irina that von Mohr "seems strong but in reality he's dangerously vulnerable. He seems calm and determined but in reality he's a weak, frustrated, lonely little man. Believing nothing, has faith in no one, loves nothing and no one. Except himself, passionately" (283). His whole interior is a soft paste of fear. Finally, then, one sees the arch-fascist as the arch-conspirator—man metamorphosed into the chilly mask which hides irrational alarm and a continuous struggle with despair. When Vincent comes to slay him, the mask breaks, and he yields in a paralysis of fear.

Somewhere between the innocent amateurs and the mutilated professionals stand the hero and heroine. Yet they are progressing toward either a mutation of personality or a breakdown such as von Mohr undergoes. The reader perceives this transition in the split between political ideal and personal desire in Irina Petrova, but one perceives it more acutely in Vincent Van der Lyn.

Prokosch calculatingly ascribes to Van der Lyn a personality entirely antipodal to von Mohr's. Where von Mohr is described as "Grecian" in the sense of being Apollonian, Vincent is portrayed as a faun. The physical appearance, however, is not for him a disguise but the truth of the inner self. Even when he is in danger, he pauses to admire the beauty of a butterfly. He instinctively contemplates life as a sensualist, as a lover. But his conspiratorial part has given him an errand. The lover of life carries the assassin's weapon, a silver paper knife. As he carries the weapon, symbolically obtained from Quintanilla, he begins to feel that he has nothing left of his former self: "Not love. Not a home. Not even friendship. Nothing except . . . He felt a cool sharp object in his pocket nestling against the palm of his hand" (185).

That the assassin's role constitutes a profound perversion of Vincent's natural instincts is emphasized by the fact that the sight of blood inevitably nauseates him. The perversion of instinct, the mutation of self, the hypnotic compulsion of the conspirator intersect to indicate the effect of war upon human beings. Prokosch envisions all mankind as betraying itself in World War II, and in much the same way that he envisions universal treachery in his frequently anthologized poem "The Conspirators." The poem says goodbye to "sweet northern music" and "the flight of the mind across the continents," for the birds will "sob for the time of man" (43, 44).

Like the poem, the novel contains a lamentation for the "sweet northern music," which one translates as "the age of reason"—the discipline and assuredness of the eighteenth century. And so, of course, Prokosch is able to use the eighteenth-century decor of Lisbon as a contrast to the spiritual dishevelment of the exiles. When Vincent peers into the casino at the Estoril, he feels that "All the bric-a-brac of a dead age hung suspended there, magically preserved, like a bee in amber" (242). Preserved or not, the aristocratic era is presumed dead. Vincent may upon occasion oppose the peace among the downtrodden and the poor with the frenetic death throes of the aristocratic past, and even feel with approbation that, in the age to follow, the peasants will rule. But at heart the novel asserts in one brilliant elegy after another that the old Europe, rotting and sinking, is in effect dead.

One might profitably compare this supposition with Arthur Koestler's similar supposition in a number of his books and in particular with *The Age of Longing* (1951). But to make this comparison is to reveal how different are the approaches of these two writers. Koestler has always been a journalist. Even his masterpiece *Darkness at Noon* (1940), for all its undeniable power, truth and influence, contains not one drop of imagination. Prokosch rests one hundred eighty degrees away from journalism. Events in the real world are of importance for the shades of feeling which they produce in him or in his characters. "Shades of feeling" may be the wrong phrase, for so momentous do the feelings sometimes become that one is uncertain as to whether they are produced by events or whether the events are occasioned by the feelings. At such moments one may well wish Prokosch were a little closer to the journalist.

Despite the excess of feeling, *The Conspirators* is an impressive achievement. Among Prokosch's novels it is more than any other patiently designed. Furthermore, it is the only one of his books that can lay claim to the unity of traditional fiction. In this one work, Prokosch appears not only to have exhausted his intuitions about war but also to have entirely satisfied them. For the subsequent novels about war—chronologically the next two, as it happens—are relatively poor performances. That *The Conspirators* represents the richest matrix of apperception and feeling is indicated by the fact that the title of the next war novel is contained in one of Quintanilla's speeches: "This war is like a fog. It fills the air we breathe . . . Every door opening, every mirror we stare at, every voice, every stranger is a link in the struggle. We've all become conspirators, every last one of us. We've all been whispering and evading and betraying. It's a new, incredible climate, like the rings of Saturn. It's the age of mist we've entered! The age of thunder"! (57-58).

II   Age of Thunder

Age of Thunder (1945), dedicated to the memory of the gallant and charming Antoine de Saint-Exupéry, opens in late May a little prior to the allied invasion of France. A young American, Jean-Nicolas Martin, is parachuted into the Haute-Savoie district of France. His instructions are to discover who has been betraying the location of the allied underground headquarters, arms deposits, and couriers in the area between Annecy and the Swiss border. He is also to make friends with the *maquis* but without revealing the nature of his own mission. Finally he is to contact a man called "Robinson" in the village of St. Pierre de Rumilly. He has been chosen for this mission because of his ability to speak German, Italian, and French and because he had lived in Geneva as a child and gone to school in St. Pierre de Rumilly. He has four days to reach the Swiss city of Monthey.

On the first night he falls in with an underground party whose members plan to cross the border. The most important members of the party are the leader Milliquet; Yernaux, a lawyer; Ulysse, a painter; Amedée, a poet; and Quivar, a Negro from Martinique. In order to avoid detection, they decide to travel by night and to rest by day. Almost immediately a fog of dubiety rises about

Milliquet. His resolve seems questionable, and he is mysteriously frightened of Quivar. On the first day, Milliquet, who has charged that one of the party is a traitor, is murdered. Martin and Quivar, who find the body in the barn where the party has sheltered itself, decide to press on on their own. (It is clear to the reader that Quivar has assassinated Milliquet, but only later is it made clear that Milliquet himself is the traitor to the underground and that he in some way is connected with Quivar's having been tortured and sexually mutilated by the Germans.) They then join a group of Italians seeking also to reach Switzerland. The party consists of an elderly mother and father, Don Giacinto and Donna Raffaelina; their adolescent son, Sebastiano; and the daughter, Susanna. They are accompanied by a cripple, Giulio. Martin falls in love with Susanna, but he and Quivar leave the Italian family when they come in sight of the Arve River.

On the same day they near the town of St. Pierre de Rumilly where Martin had lived as a child. Leaving Quivar in hiding, Martin enters the town. At the inn he meets the mysterious Robinson, evidently a betrayer, who turns him over to the German police and to the even more mysterious "K. M." Incredibly, K. M., after a philosophical discourse, releases him; and Martin leaves the town. He is, however, unable to find Quivar. Later he finds his body. He has been killed by irresponsible *maquisards*. After two encounters with the *maquis*, during which another traitor is disclosed and executed, the underground camp is attacked by German planes; and Martin wakes, wounded, in a monastery whither the Italian family has also come. In a depressingly sentimental scene Martin consummates his love with Susanna. In an even more outrageous scene the hideously mutilated Giulio attempts to murder the hero out of envy of Martin's ability to command the love of a woman! Despite the lovers' bliss and Giulio's blight, Martin and Susanna, hand in hand, cross on the fourth day the border into Switzerland.

It is, of course, unfair to summarize the action of a novel; for summaries—divorced from the metaphors, the tone and characterization—always sound worse than the book itself. Even so, *Age of Thunder* is almost as embarrassing as this summary. There is something curious about the whole work. Noting that the novel is nearly as severe in its time boundaries as *The Conspirators* and noting also that it follows the cherished journey formula which usually inspires Prokosch to excel, one wonders what went wrong.

There are two fundamental tactical errors; but, before examining them, it is helpful to consider the position which this novel occupies in Prokosch's career. *Age of Thunder* is Prokosch's sixth novel. In each of the previous five he had taken a somewhat different approach, though all remain easily within his idiom. In *Age of Thunder* he again attempted a variation and, as it turned out, a disastrous one. He changed the nature of his hero within the journey formula. Jean-Nicolas Martin is not the nice modest boy of *Night of the Poor,* nor the self-effacing hero of *The Asiatics.* He enters as a participator into the dynamics of the strange events. Whereas the hero of *The Asiatics* becomes at most a rather tenderhearted and tolerant satirist of the passions or vanities of the exotic characters and events, Jean-Nicolas helps to create the events, becoming as a result both more real and less acceptable. Instead of the reader's joining one who acutely observes and vicariously experiences exoticisms in exotic places, the reader grows aware that Jean-Nicolas is himself an exotic. When that happens, the foibles, the vanity, and the silly passions too much accrue to the hero; and he receives the reader's satire, neither tenderhearted nor tolerant. Instead of a narrator who mirrors the antics of others, Jean-Nicolas all too opaquely joins in the antics.

Perhaps Prokosch decided to make Jean-Nicolas an active rather than a passive hero because an active hero had worked out well in *The Conspirators.* But *The Conspirators* is not a picaresque novel. It employs very few characters and only one who is really bizarre. In addition Van der Lyn's mission seems both inevitable and important while Jean-Nicolas' tour of the Haute-Savoie is pretty haphazard. It is hard to believe that anything at all is at stake. From such lacks rises the second flaw. Against the background of the war and the seriousness of the issue, Jean-Nicolas' wanderings seem a dreamy trifling with important matters. Perhaps great war novels can only be written by strict realists. An André Malraux or an Ernest Hemingway does not neglect the dull problems of logistics.

One grieves that he must condemn *Age of Thunder,* for it begins brilliantly, and some of the scenes stand with Prokosch's best. Often the events ascend to a real unreality which is splendidly faithful to the hypnotic atmospheres of war. Here is an illustration: Quivar shoots some German soldiers who have playfully stripped off their clothes and ridden their horses into a stream. Before the shooting the soldiers are described as follows:

> They were scooping handfuls of water over the horses, soaking the horses' heads and manes. Everywhere there was a splashing of water; the drops leapt and sparkled in the wild red sunlight. Everywhere the air shone with glittering red sprays, and there was a strange timorous exultation in the air; only the boys' faces remained solemn; even their smiles were intent and solemn.

Then:

> The shots rang out in rapid succession. Jean-Nicolas looked down among the birches. The scene froze instantaneously. The water stopped splashing and the singing stopped. The horses and the soldiers stopped moving altogether. Nothing moved until one of the German soldiers slipped slowly from his horse into the water, without a sound almost and without a splash" (56-57).

Such a passage dives deep into the curious dissociation of act and will in war, dives deeper into the emotional truth of war than the whole of Norman Mailer's *The Naked and the Dead.* But there are not enough such passages in *Age of Thunder* to save it.

In spite of its all-too-evident badness, *Age of Thunder* is of interest for its hints at the primitivistic direction in Prokosch's later works as well as for its re-assessments of earlier positions. Quivar's characterization appears to provide the work sheets for the primitivism of *Storm and Echo* (1948). And Jean-Nicolas Martin voices a toughening of Prokosch's attitudes. "Happiness" does not come so easily to him as it does for the hero of *The Asiatics* who is content to merge with the richness and timelessness of the moment. For Jean-Nicolas the concept of happiness is more nearly the poetic masochism found in Keats's "Ode on Melancholy": "I feel," he tells Susanna, "a strange sharp happiness in knowing that what I have I have only for a time, and that everything must die . . . Yes, more and more I feel this, Susanna. The leaves look greener every year; the clouds look whiter; and when I think that soon I will never see them again, the pines smell more spicy and the flight of birds looks more dazzling than ever before. I keep saying to myself: there, there it is; soon it will be gone forever. And then a fever grips me, Susanna, and I can hardly tell whether it is despair or happiness. I call it happiness" (130).

Of greater moment in a study of Prokosch, *Age of Thunder* offers a less pessimistic reaction to World War II than does *The Conspirators*. True, the impression that the old order is being swept away continues. True, there is the suggestion that the war will last long beyond the time when the killing stops. At the same time the impression arises that Prokosch no longer feels that the war is tantamount to the decline and fall of everything. When Amedée wonders for what they are all suffering, the lawyer Yernaux observes in a long speech that they are suffering for the sake of freedom. "I would rather be a humble cobbler in Lichtenstein," he adds, "than a Komissar in the most resplendent autocracy in Europe" (38). Nor does Prokosch appear to find the war quite so unforgivable and unbearable. One character compares it to a "purification" (205); another says that the war is "a colossal surgical operation" (239).

The concern with freedom as a value takes a curious bend in Prokosch's thinking, for he does not very much believe that true freedom of action or will exist. Freedom becomes, therefore, the right "to explore and illuminate" one's life. Freedom also becomes "the right to tragedy. . . . Tragedy is a kind of ecstasy, or exaltation . . . it is the final acknowledgment of man's dignity" (50-51).

That Prokosch seriously advances this notion of the right to tragedy is proven by the fact that he also seriously questions it. For the idea parallels the rationalizations of Nazi agent K. M., who believes that for Germany "humanitarianism constituted a deadly peril, compromise an insidious trap, culture a mask." Despite the cold horror of these words, K. M. can also believe that "To know how fleeting are the awards of courage, how ironical and lonely the rewards of wisdom . . . is what it means to become an individual" (167-68). Now, K. M.'s belief is only a rancid extension of the right to tragedy. Still, this very extension, this exaggeration, is a stroke of subtle irony worthy of Ibsen; for, like Ibsen in *The Wild Duck*, Prokosch is affirming his concept by arguing against its being carried too far. The right to tragedy, or the association of freedom with tragedy, is repeated with more insistence but with less hope in *The Idols of the Cave*.

III The Idols of the Cave

The Idols of the Cave (1946), a long, greatly ramified novel, is confined in locale to New York City. The mood and the kinds of characters bear obvious kinship with the more or less "realistic" and "social" novels, *The Skies of Europe* and *A Ballad of Love*. It would not have been improper to have considered it alongside them. However, the novel spans the years between 1941 and 1945, and it leans heavily on the circumambient war for its motor power, as well as for its philosophical distractions. Furthermore, if many of the characters are cut from the same cloth as those in these other novels, their grotesque feelings and their behavior reflect the intensity and fever of the war's violence.

Like the Lisbon of *The Conspirators*, New York during the war offered a refuge to exiles. These exiles were often the moneyed, cultured aristocrats of Europe. They brought with them their standards of excellence, their own ideals and prejudices. They were as alien an intrusion into New York as the Fifth Army was in Naples. They formed their own circles, often brilliant ones; started journals; and inspired cafes. The exiles are drawn with verve and truth. Some appear to be caricatures of actual people. Indeed, when one "fashionable" young English poet is described briefly, he is wittily named Hubert Marsden. One readily recognizes the description to be that of W. H. Auden (202).

To this milieu, Jonathan Ely, an American student of architecture, returns in 1941 after several years abroad in Bordeaux, Barcelona, and Lisbon. He finds himself partly drawn into the world of the exiles and partly into that of relatives and old friends, most of whom share with him a Yale background. These two sets counterpoint each other insofar as they involve essentially disastrous love affairs which bloom like forced flowers in greenhouses. The petals open under fluorescent lights and in controlled temperatures. Jonathan's own love affair with Ukrainian, ballet-dancer Lydia Illanova is basically a humiliating pursuit of an iridescent but promiscuous butterfly. For a time, matters between the lovers progress fairly smoothly; but Jonathan is drafted. And, when he returns on leave to New York, he sees that she is incapable of fidelity. At the same time his mother, who has long lived in London, comes to New York where she dies. At length he breaks with Lydia and falls in love with Delia Potter, the wife of his cousin Quincy. But this love comes to nothing, is not even expressed; for Delia has in the meantime fallen in love with Pierre Maillard, a young French painter and a friend of Jonathan's. Delia, who has left her husband, cannot face even normal difficulties in her affair with Pierre. She eventually commits suicide, and Pierre, the war being over, returns to Europe, as do the rest of the expatriates.

Inasmuch as the haste and breathlessness, the neuroses and weak sins of the characters are blamed on the wartime atmosphere of New York, it is appropriate that the city itself should receive considerable detailing. One can point to scores of writers capable of offering a more balanced and natural portrait of New York; but, when it comes to extracting the essence of a scene, Frederic Prokosch has no masters and few equals. The city, reproduced like a *trompe-l'oeil* painting, with a sinister depth and clarity, broods over the story. Its perennial, heartless magnificence glares at the reader. Its staggering human artifice and, even more staggering, its artifice without humanity form at the back of the perspective while the particularity of the time moves to the foreground. The petulant world of the exiles, both pitiable and disquieting moves toward the eye, creating what Prokosch calls a "certain hothouse flavor" (11). To be sure, the Europeans are like plants shifted from their natural settings to be pampered but never pleased in some outrageous botanical station.

Even more sharply highlighted is the somnambulistic jungle of movement and transience which characterized New York during the war. In one wide-angle shot, Prokosch almost too cruelly captures the illicit pageantry of Broadway in 1943:

The half-darkness added a tense and mysterious gaiety to the street. It was like a carnival scene, with a dazzling variety of gowns and uniforms, passing through the unending stream of faces. And over it all hung the darkness of war, which gave them an air of anonymity, of masquerade. . . .

The soldiers and sailors were rolling brightly, like pebbles, through the promiscuous tangle of civilians. . . . Nothing here seemed surprising. No one looked out of place. All taboos were abolished; all the barriers were obliterated. Every eccentricity of face, dress, desire had been flung into the onrush. A kind of hordelike fatalism pervaded the scene. It had the air of some vast Asiatic migration (157).

With the help of such panoramic views, the sense of the city cements the novel together. At the same time, alas, it overpowers the action and dwarfs the characters. The characters often strain one's patience; they feel too often and too much. They continually comment on each other's appearance, with the result, apparently, that, in the span of four or five years, they inordinately age.

Though the story is told from a multiple point of view, most of it is told through Jonathan Ely; and he clearly is the main character. To the initiated reader it is also clear that he is a Prokosch hero par excellence. Like the youth in *The Asiatics*, he has the odd streak of white across the center of his hair. And, were he wandering in fantastic Asia, one feels assured that he would modestly tolerate every wickedness and every virtue in his proper study of mankind. As the hero, however, who inhabits a normal world, he is victimized by those whom he loves. The humility which seems strength in a world of improbables seems, if not weakness, a sad plight in the world of ordinary relationships.

Lydia Illanova also has her counterparts in *The Skies of Europe* and in *A Ballad of Love* whose heroines are also dancers and who, like Lydia, have attractive moles on their faces. Like the others, she is atrociously selfish, atrociously vital, and an astonishing tramp. She demands absolute obeisance from Jonathan. "Think only of me," she says to Jonathan. "Don't think of the rest of the world" (65). She is never so pleased as when she stimulates sexual longing in others—and then she smiles to herself like an archaic Aphrodite. Jonathan sees her as "a kind of distillation of the city." His submission to her he sees as "a symbolical act of obedience to the city's own hypnotic power" (67). These two phrases suggest to what extent the city is a dominant character in the story. And they suggest as well how tired, guilty, and impossible—like Tennyson's Lancelot and Guinevere—these lovers are. And, like Tennyson's adulterers, they are only believable as separate entities; as lovers they are quite incredible. And so, in the end, the minor characters may seem to the reader more finely turned. Likewise, Pierre Maillard may seem more interesting than Jonathan Ely.

Pierre is intricate and asymmetrical. He is selfish and ambitious but not to the degree that Lydia is. He is covert but not really two-faced, though one side of his face (like Gouipilliere's in *The Seven Who Fled*) is a little different from the other side. He is sexually ambivalent and has loved, perhaps still loves, Jonathan; but that side of his nature (or of his face) is not clearly seen, except for hints about minor erotic adventures. Despite his shadiness, one does not doubt that he will always land like a cat on his feet. One is also sure that fragile Delia will break.

Delia, entirely good and trusting, turns to Pierre only partly because her husband is a dull man, middle-aged at thirty-three. She turns to Pierre largely because the war shakes her life, secretly touching it with a sense of change and impermanence. But, because her nature is basically puritanical, she cannot forgive herself and must indeed begin to punish herself and Pierre as soon as they become lovers. Her guilt demands unhappiness and eventually self-destruction. In this whole relationship, Prokosch demonstrates an acute understanding of the two characters. One could advance Pierre's and Delia's ill-fated affair as a classical case history of love in wartime. The puritan disposition is weak and vulnerable in the milieu of wartime license; yet, at the same time, it is strong in its ability to take refuge in the recesses of personality, there to wait for its revenge. Though Delia is the only puritan in the novel, she is not alone in possessing a divided self. For the emergence of a hidden personality is woven into the whole design of the novel.

In this respect, the title of the novel is instructive. Prokosch himself helpfully directs us to Francis Bacon's *Novum Organum*: "The Idols of the Cave are the idols of the individual man. For every one (besides the errors common to human nature in general) has a cave or den of his own, which refracts and discolors the light of nature. . . . So that the spirit of man is in fact a thing variable and full of perturbation, and governed as it were by chance." But Prokosch does not have in mind exactly the same self-delusions that Bacon did. Rather Prokosch associates the idol with animality—sometimes seriously, sometimes comically. When Jonathan and Lydia visit the zoo in Central Park, they gaze at two hippopotamuses who are named Rose and Schlemil and who obviously satirize the two lovers. But the grossness and sentimentality of Rose and Schlemil contrast with the noble lion who roars with passion when Lydia and Jonathan are happy together. Later on, when Jonathan perceives the counterpoint of their affair with Delia's and Pierre's, the lion roars with immense boredom. The zoo imagery, while not ponderous, appears at significant moments throughout the novel. At the end Jonathan goes alone to the zoo; and, at this point, the imagery joins hands with the title to effect a theme. The animals are confined in cages, they are in dens, but they are stirring as if in a dim apprehension of some freedom to come. Yet the reader does not quite see why the novel needs to be concerned with animal instinct, or with an animal personality confined but straining to free itself. As a matter of fact, he has to wait for Prokosch's next novel *Storm and Echo* to find out why Prokosch is concerned with the atavistic aspect, of life. And when he does find out, he sees, what is not at all clear in *Idols of the Cave*: the lion that roars in his cage has some connection with Prokosch's view of man as an evolving, historical creature.

World War II solved some problems for Prokosch and created others. He had, prior to the conflict, always contemplated the possibility of war as if it were the approach of doomsday. When war came and then went, and man and his problems persisted, Prokosch lost some of the basis for his world outlook, for his delicious fears. Of the three novels set in the war years, only *The Conspirators* is successful, and the reason for its success is relatively clear. But it is not, finally, a good book because it is better unified or better conceived. It is a good book because Prokosch's old view of the collapse of Europe and civilization remained valid in the immune atmosphere of neutral Portugal. One did not in the first two years of the war know what would happen to Europe. As the war continued, however, it became evident that some new beginning, rather than all the once-anticipated Ragnaroks, must eventually ensue. Both *Age of Thunder* and *The Idols of the Cave* are seeking for a new beginning or, better, for a new approach to the destiny of man. In *The Idols of the Cave* only the most tentative notions rise as to what the new approach might be. But one spies from time to time a fear of mechanization and of conformity in the western world. These tentative notions, however, became positive focuses in later novels.

CHAPTER 6

The Landscape of the Soul

I *Innocence and Evil:* Night of the Poor *and*
A Tale for Midnight

TO UNDERSTAND Frederic Prokosch's best work, one must understand his worst. The present chapter seeks entry into a pattern involving both. This is not to say that Prokosch's strengths are created by his weaknesses; it is to say that his heights emerge as a result of his whole geography's being pinched together, as if by a geological catastrophe, within the limitations of his perspective. Two novels, the early *Night of the Poor* (1939) and the relatively late *A Tale for Midnight* (1955), mark out the limitations.

Night of the Poor aims at combining a story of an innocent youth's experience with an allegory of America rendered bitter and aimless by the economic depression of the 1930's. The political symbolism is hinted at by a quotation from Walt Whitman:

> Have the past struggles succeeded?
> What has succeeded? yourself? your nation? Nature?
> Now understand me well—it is preserved in the essence of things that from any fruition of success, no matter what, shall come forth something to make a greater struggle necessary.

In *Night of the Poor* the boy's groping toward maturity and understanding embodies the notion of youthful America which now must also put aside pioneer frontiers like childish things and grow up. One is not, however, much concerned with the allegorical aspect of the novel for the reason that the story of the boy never goes well enough for one to worry about what it means.

The boy, Tom, after the death of an uncle in Wisconsin, hitchhikes toward his parents' home in Texas through Illinois, Indiana, Kentucky, Tennessee, and Mississippi. On the way he encounters lust, poverty, murder, and a lynching. He meets Americans who have lost in the depression their self-respect, as well as others who have maintained it. He meets wicked boys, a gangster, a sad mystical Negro, and the inevitable good-hearted prostitute. The important characters are Sandy, a tragic little boy who dies, and Lucy, a Midwestern Rima, whom he loves, loses, and finds again in Texas. Every so often the novel pauses to roll off American place names, making the reader feel trapped in a celestial depot. Sometimes *Night of the Poor* reads as if Prokosch were trying to bring *Huckleberry Finn* up to date by adding a drop of Whitman and a soupçon of D. H. Lawrence, all mixed in well with his own assortment of oracular eccentrics.

But it is not merely, as Schorer pointed out, that the realism and fantasy will not fuse.[1] Far more significantly, the progress of the innocent is repugnant. Tom comes to the reader a shy, "good" boy. He evinces a proper Huck Finn horror of cruelty. He responds with tenderness and love to the frail Sandy and to Sandy's Uncle Waldo. All in all, one is led to expect that his experience, his growing up, will be important for the reason that good will come of it. But all that does emerge, finally, is a sexual awakening consummated by copulation. At the outset of the novel an embarrassingly tasteless scene occurs when a centaur-like character says to Tom: "You ain't never had it. . . . It feels mighty good, Tom. . . . It cleans you out. . . . Don't worry you'll have it some day, Tom" (36). Even earlier, when in an old shack Tom inspects the lurid graffiti on the walls, he finds "an element sensuous and exciting in the thick, woody, private smell that drenched the place," and his reaction is a quickening of the pulse (27).

Now, the objection to these and other similar scenes does not involve a question of realism or probability; it involves what these scenes do to the character of Tom. They ally him with the spirit of pornography, which always insists on the speedy corruption of the innocents; they never imply retribution or sorrow or societal disapproval. As a consequence, having des-

troyed the primary innocence in the character, Prokosch can
never convince his reader of Tom's innocence or goodness in any
other respect. Ultimately, the reader knows that innocence
bores Prokosch deeply. Or, to put it in a more relevant way,
Prokosch, lacking belief in a philosophic concept of innocence,
is barred from this romantic concept in his romantically fur-
bished fiction. The deprivation is greater for him than for a
writer like Henry Fielding because Prokosch focuses on individuals, on their inner awareness, and on the soul possessed
by demonic strife. But what is the purpose of such a strife
where innocence has already gone by default? A consonant
limitation appears in *A Tale for Midnight*.

A Tale for Midnight seems to have no aims beyond what
Prokosch claims for it. "This is a new type of book for me: a
novel based on historical fact and involving considerable research, yet at the same time my first novel to be dedicated
wholly to narrative, to storytelling per se and above all."[2] The
story of the murder of Count Francesco Cenci in 1599 under
the pontificate of Clement VIII is well known. The count, after
a dissolute life, developed an irrepressible hatred toward his
children. His daughter Beatrice, following fruitless attempts to
escape from her situation, finally conspired with her stepmother
Lucrezia and her brothers to murder Cenci with the help of
hired assassins. The job was not a tidy one. Suspicions arose,
and, with the aid of cross-examination and torture, the facts became clear. Lucrezia and Beatrice, together with Beatrice's
brother Giacomo, were executed.

Shelley, in his play *The Cenci* (1819), took the view that the
count had used Beatrice incestuously, thus justifying the murder
in an emotional sense, while intellectually insisting that Beatrice
should not have met evil with evil. Prokosch follows a different
interpretation: namely, that the alleged incest, technically un-
true, was a desperate ploy devised by her lawyer. Her reasons for
murder were, Prokosch feels, a general reaction against the
count's cruelty and a specific fear of his discovering that she
was pregnant by the seneschal of the provincial castle where
the count kept Lucrezia and Beatrice virtually imprisoned.
However, one or two phosphorescent scenes occur, implying a
vague incestuous feeling on the part of the count, but there

are no definite acts. Anyway, his tastes, according to Prokosch, run more to shepherds and stable boys than to daughters. No matter what interpretation, the story is apt to jerk and grimace with the gestures of Gothic melodrama. To Prokosch's credit, he does not overplay the aspects of the Grand Guignol. On the contrary, the murder occurs in the first section of the novel, and the main interest lies in the Dostoievskian unraveling of the crime and in the effect of it upon Beatrice. This effect is often brilliantly detailed and nowhere better than in one scene where Beatrice inspects the toys which had belonged to a childhood now severed from her adult corruption: "She . . . peered at the row of bedraggled little dolls. Their wax faces were blurred with years of desertion. There was a desperate air about them; they were begging for recognition. . . . She caught sight of a doll that she herself had fondled years ago. . . . She pressed the doll to her breast and whispered: 'Constanza . . . my poor little darling'" (165-66).

Despite such moments of pathos, there is something oddly inhuman about *A Tale for Midnight*. The story, of course, is inhuman, but Prokosch converts a story which bubbles with as much evil as *Macbeth* into a story possessing no evil at all. One has to admire his accomplishment, for few writers would have wanted to or have been able to manage it. Prokosch does so because he imbues Beatrice with an absolute compulsion, an absolute obsession, nay, an absolute necessity to kill her father. She moves like an implacable tide over other characters. Neither Lucrezia nor the seneschal Olympio has any real desire to murder Count Francesco, but they are powerless before Beatrice. Nor is it at all a matter of will power, for Beatrice has no will. Her nature has become that of a murderess entirely outside what her will might be. If she moves with the power of a tide, she also moves as does a tide in response to the calendar. Even after the murder is done, after she thinks to gather her being together, she still thinks to save herself, we find: "Her silhouette, dark and featureless, hung in the octagonal mirror. The tension, the dread were invisible. All she saw was a shaggy head, like an ape's, slightly bowed, as though in obedience to some inexorable law in her being" (141).

Curiously, however, though we should expect such dominance

to generate power, there is none. There is no power because
Beatrice has gone beyond will. She has become, as the shaggy
ape's head implies, like a natural law. In so doing, Beatrice has
also gone beyond evil. What is true of Beatrice is also true of all
of Prokosch's embodiments of wicked behavior. The behavior
becomes behaviorism; the characters drift in a compulsion beyond their volition. They are not powerful, they are not tragic,
they are not capable of evil. So, though one cannot say that
Prokosch is insensitive to good or bad conduct, one must say
that he does not conceive the cosmos as split between forces of
good and evil. He does not *philosophically* conceive of innocence
and evil.

What is left, then, for Prokosch in his region, pushed in upon
itself by these strange limitations of the frontiers? The inexorable
law of being is left. And, in obedience to this law, his finest work
has come forward. These are his novels founded upon his belief
in fulfilling the law of one's being, in fulfilling one's destiny.
Seeing the intensity of this preoccupation, we apprehend the
ambivalence of his passion for "freedom"; for, though the individual is not "free," he must still possess freedom in order to
fulfill himself.

II *The Country for Old Men*

Frederic Prokosch's second novel, *The Seven Who Fled*
(1937), opens in the very center of Asia with a party fleeing
a political disturbance in Kashgar. The party is stopped at
Aqsu by authorities who decide to hold two members as hostages
and to jail two others. One other who is ill stays in Aqsu. The
others are permitted to continue toward their destination,
Hwang-Ho. The bulk of the novel pursues the fates of the
seven Europeans who came to Aqsu. Their fates, both similar
and different, eventually establish a pattern and meaning.

Anthony Layeville, a tall, handsome Englishman, continues
on with Dr. Liu's caravan; but he later joins another caravan
going to Shigatse in Tibet. He realizes his folly but he is mag-
netized by the icy summits of the mountains. "But above all,
something in himself . . . something intense that scarcely ever
revealed itself in him, but which really underlay everything

he felt and did," draws him on (50). Layeville's caravan eventually becomes lost and snowbound and all die.

Over and over again the reader learns that some cold intellectuality lies at the center of Layeville. So that on first consideration his ultimate death in Tibetan snow seems an appropriate end for him. But while this symbology holds true in a general way, the story is considerably complicated by Layeville's memories of his earlier life and by his relationship with the Turgot, Tansang.

Tansang, the son of a wealthy merchant, tells Layeville that at seventeen he had killed his cousin, that at nineteen he "had handled serpents and walked among the wolves . . . At twenty-one he escaped from a burning vessel . . . at twenty-three he came near drowning . . . at twenty-five he had been sick with cholera . . . and had cured himself by bathing in ice-cold water" (52). His twenty-seven years have been harsh but adventurous. The relationship between Layeville and Tansang is a mixture, on each side, of attraction and repellence. Layeville at times feels as if the hardness and "secret violence" of Tansang are "like a hot iron cauterizing the bite of a snake" (68). At other times, he fears and hates him. That Tansang feels the same attraction and the same disgust is indicated by his behavior which counterpoints amity with hostility, loquaciousness with sullen silence and evasion.

Despite fear and hostility, as the men in the snowbound caravan sicken and begin to die, Layeville feels that he must save Tansang's life, that to do so would be to "save himself" (80). Indeed, to save Tansang would be to save himself, for the two personalities are held together by a force which makes of them an identity. Each realizes in the other the self which he is not, yet seeks to be. They are opposite selves who, like the souls of the lovers Aristophanes mentions in *The Symposium*, seek each other throughout life. The awareness of this relationship sharpens as Layeville, dying of exposure and malnutrition, thinks of his past.

Layeville's remembrance of things past reveals a life in England characterized by a puritanical, protected childhood, one which leads to his ambivalent student days at Cambridge and then to his restless journeys in search of an unknown goal.

The Cambridge memories, detailed in exquisite prose, reveal Layeville's early surrender to a group of hypersensitive friends, who create a separate world of delicate relationships, blooming like fey orchids in a humid rain forest. At Cambridge, his life is "consummated too early—too romantically, too exhaustingly" (96) in the extravagant, electrically charged atmosphere of homophylic friendships. As a consequence of the early consummation, he turns for a time to what one guesses is a period of sexual promiscuity in Berlin, followed by a desire for purity in the Greek Islands; this is followed in turn by expeditions to Africa, Arabia and Turkestan. He has learned in England, "that declining and dingy land of adorable scenes and adorable faces, . . . not to care too much; not to fidget, to fret, to resent, to loathe . . . little by little he learned, like a true Englishman, not to care too deeply" (97). Indeed, he has "lost, somewhere amongst the ardors of childhood and youth, all power to love" (99).

One hesitates, faintly amused and faintly aghast. The portrait of Layeville, to anyone who has read, say, Christopher Isherwood's novels, is obviously a collage of a particular literary generation which came to maturity in England in the 1930's. But the portrait also balloons to represent England in a larger, historical sense—as decadent and, indeed, despite all of its charm, sterile. For the word "sterile" must finally advance as the term most descriptive of Layeville himself. When he thinks that if he can save Tansang's life, he can save himself, the meaning is that, if he could bring naturalness and violence, hence love, into his life, he could save himself. It is, after all, Tansang who says to him that Layeville is "a very strange man" because he is "so full of love, so full of kindness and wisdom, and even courage, and none of it used" (79). Because none of his virtue is used and because Tansang dies, Layeville at the end can only see snow, sterile and cold as himself, as his narcissistic destiny. It looks "dear" to him, "desirable," and "intimate" (103). He has failed then to find and embrace his anti-self, Tansang. And Tansang, who, if he is natural and loving, nevertheless lacks the virtues of intellect and civilization, has equally failed to come to terms with his anti-self.

A similar but hardly identical pairing aligns the characters of the Russian Serafimov and the Belgian Goupillière, who are detained in an inn at Aqsu as hostages. Whereas Layeville and Tansang counterpoise over-civilization and primitive sensibility, Serafimov and Goupillière form antitheses of animal innocence and civilized ruthlessness.

Serafimov, who has escaped from years of enforced labor in Siberia after having been arrested with some student intellectuals in Odessa, contains in his great, embarrassed body an utterly sweet but inarticulate soul. Though he possesses a sure sensitivity to values, he cannot deal with the world, nor can he begin to understand himself. In his own reverie about his youth in Dolya, Russia, he does not perceive that in his love for a girl there exists "subtle imperfection" (146).[3] The imperfection derives from her being more worldly than he.

Contrasting with Serafimov's life, Goupillière's has been remarkably labyrinthine. The bastard son of a murdered servant girl, he has as a child compensated for this disgrace by becoming more clever than his schoolmates. His very name, which contains the French word for "fox," insists on his cunning. His neurotic self-magnification leads him to a precocious awareness of good and evil and ultimately into an adulthood where he steals in order to continue to believe in his superiority. He steals love, as well as trinkets and furs, but all for the same reason. Eventually, however, he begins to long not "for physical love, but for spiritual love. For power over the souls of people. For the power, in short, to corrupt the human heart" (195). He has, one sees, become a narcissist. In theological terms, he has fallen into the sin of self-love or of pride. Finally, he murders a prostitute who has taunted him, but not before she has destroyed the beauty of his face with a pair of scissors. Significantly the scar divides his face between beauty and ugliness. The scar also changes his life. He feels unlucky now and fearful. Like Satan, he becomes an outcast and a wanderer.

Though one observes that the relationship between Goupillière and Serafimov is allegorically that of an angel and a fiend, one does not in reality find that Serafimov is a seraph or that Goupillière is a devil. For Serafimov is too much a relativist to be deific, and Goupillière's egotism is too much explained by his childhood conditioning to represent an abstract power of evil. The symbology of seraph and fiend, then, does not destroy the basic relationship of the innocent animal and the ruthlessly civilized man.

Once again, as with Layeville and Tansang, a tension of attraction and repugnance arises between Serafimov and Goupillière. The tension builds when Serafimov falls strangely in love with Madame Tastin, an aging prostitute of the city. Goupillière visits Madame Tastin upon occasion with a detached, cynical amusement that infuriates Serafimov. Yet it is more because of the antagonisms of self than because of jealousy that Serafimov decides he must kill Goupillière—as a matter of sacred duty. For the same reason, Goupillière instinctively comprehends that Serafimov obsessively desires to annihilate him. In the end Serafimov pursues Goupillière at night to a ruined tower on the outskirts of the town. Goupillière waits inside the enclosure. Serafimov stumbles at the top of the wall and falls. When Goupillière thinks him dead, he feels "despair":

> He rose and walked across to Serafimov. He knelt beside him, gazed upon his closed eyelids, touched his warm wet pock-marked forehead. There was a deep gash in his forehead. He felt the warm blood clinging to his finger tips. A terrible longing filled his heart. And instantly he understood that this unbelievable moment was of course the closest he had ever come to self-forgetfulness; to reality, real fear, and real devotion. In fact, what he felt for one inexplicable instant was almost a kind of adoration (213).

But then Goupillière remembers that Serafimov had had the habit of looking at an object kept in his pocket. In a return of his fiend-like curiosity, he searches for the object, which, as it happens, is a token of Serafimov's early, idealistic love for the girl in Dolya. Serafimov, however, is not dead. When Goupillière becomes aware that he is still alive, he does not try to save himself but waits for Serafimov to revive and kill him. With a smile he awaits his "martyrdom" and the act which will make his life "complete" (215).

Again, then, we have a story of opposed personalities which ought to be reconciled but cannot be. If Serafimov possesses unworldliness, his unworldliness is on the side of an ox-like stupidity. If Goupillière possesses worldly knowledge, his knowledge limits him within himself—even drives him at the end to welcome death as a martyrdom. And Serafimov's urgency to destroy his anti-self is of further interest. Were it a matter of good destroying evil, we, as well as Serafimov, would be the happier for it. Such, evidently, is not the case; for, in destroying Goupillière, he himself becomes a fallen angel. In the "Epilogue" he reappears, drunkenly proclaiming that he has been "saved" (477). But his face is that of "a ruined hero," and he now bears a great scar on his forehead, the result of his "fall" in the tower. The division in Goupillière has been, it seems, transplanted. However, Serafimov's last words indicate that he has learned something, though what he has learned is not angelic dogma but the art of worldly wisdom: "Everything, remember, is forgivable. . . . For all of it springs from love, however it may appear. . . . Man is eternally imperfect, the mercy of God is boundless. There is nothing that cannot be forgiven" (478).

The next pair of anti-selves, those of German Hugo Wildenbruch, and of Austrian Joachim von Wald, introduces another variation in the formula. The two young geologists are confined in a prison in Aqsu, reminiscent of another prison in *The Asiatics,* where the hardships bring out the best and the worst in people. Still, one learns more about them after they escape and come by way of caravan into a little hidden valley in Mongolia, where they spend the winter as the guests of a mysterious Russian, Mordovinov.

Once again the difference between the two is one of the angelic versus the satanic, and again, the terms "angelic" and "satanic" are relative rather than absolute. Wildenbruch, whose name, "savage-flaw," is surely allegorical, presents a case history of a Germany that is losing its humanity and its rationality as it veers off in search of a führer. In Hugo Wildenbruch's memory of his childhood, one learns that he deplored his mother's sweet, tubercular weakness and admired his uncle's cold-eyed hardness. He worships, among his friends, those who are "heroic" in the sense of courting hardship and developing muscles. He believes in ambition, discipline, and above all, in "feeling." Even though he is a scientist, science seems to him of little importance beside vague, heroic emotion.

Joachim Von Wald, whose sylvan name readily contrasts with the name "Wildenbruch," enters the novel as the incarnation of goodness. His blond beauty is described as "angelic" (249). The reader is also told that there "was nothing subtle or inverted here; his heart was still a mirror, pure and simple" (11). In addition to possessing a symbolic valence, Von Wald also assumes the consciousness of the typical Prokoschean wanderhero:

> Two longings had, all his life long, lain warm in him: that for a home, and that for a distant land: that for the gentle past, in other words, and that for the exciting future. But how, he wondered, form out of these two a single desire? So that little by little the past might assume lucidity, the present grow meaningful and stirring, the future fall into place, and time lie so controlled by the spirit that neither past, present nor future should ever grow totally possessive, and that instead they might become harmonious, single, substantial, mature (312).

One is not likely to find a better statement of Prokosch's view of life. In fact, as one examines Von Wald's character further, he finds that his instincts are those of an artist rather than of a geologist. His meditation of the past grows into "a condensation of all profound experience" (311). He investigates life through private symbols that are created to give order to the clutter of existence.

Wildenbruch and Von Wald, however, do not exist in an antipathetic relationship, as do the previous characters. Their personalities remain merged in an almost mystical comity until the winter in Mordovinov's cottage. Here, as Wildenbruch fights against his tuberculosis—his inner weakness in other words, over which he throws a disguise of disciplined hardness —the two personalities diverge. When Wildenbruch contemplates Von Wald's innocence, he momentarily feels an envy, a hostility. He decides that Von Wald needs to be "more disciplined, more intent, more ambitious" (249). Likewise in the revealing light of duress and Asia, Joachim Von Wald comes to realize both how close he is to Wildenbruch and also how separate from him. When at length both of them manage to get to Shanghai, Von Wald says goodbye to Wildenbruch and wonders, "what will become of you? Good-bye, good-bye, for I'll never see you again!" (474). The implication is obvious. Von Wald, even as he experiences sorrow on leaving his friend, must dissociate himself from an alter ego which would destroy him. For, beneath Wildenbruch's severe armor, beneath his romantic hero-worship, beneath even his tell-tale illness, he nurses a death-wish. His very struggles against death bring him closer to it. Hence, in separating from Wildenbruch, Von Wald saves his being; and, since his being is essentially spiritual, one can say that he saves his soul.

A final variation on the central theme of *The Seven Who Fled* appears in the story of Olivia and Paul de la Scaze. The variation almost exceeds variation and, for a bit, seems to break from the choreography of anti-selves. Olivia and Paul are less dramatically opposed than Layeville and Tansang, Serafimov and Goupillière or Von Wald and Wildenbruch. They have in common a background of frustration or of unused energies. Yet they also possess a crucial dissimilarity.

Their stories are told separately, but all the same they are ineluctably intertwined. Olivia Barrios, who is Spanish, has never found love though she has made sexual liaisons. She meets and marries the older, wealthy de la Scaze in Mallorca. No particular reason can be found on her side to account for the marriage. She does not love de la Scaze and soon she begins to dislike him. Cold, disgruntled, disappointed with each other, they wander in Asia. In Aqsu, when de la Scaze is too ill to travel, she abandons him and goes on with Dr. Liu's caravan. On the journey she becomes ill, and Dr. Liu takes her to his home in Lu-Chow. Here, as she regains strength, she begins to be afraid that Dr. Liu is holding her captive. Finally, she flees and manages to obtain passage to Shanghai on a river boat. Fever and a continuous (symbolic) menstruation weaken her on the long journey down the Yangtse. At various stops, however, her awareness of the swarming horror and beauty of humanity grows. In particular she becomes fascinated with the hordes of prostitutes. Finally the owner of the boat sells Olivia into a house of prostitution in Shanghai. She herself offers no more resistance to this destiny than does Goupillière to his death at the hands of

Serafimov. The meaning of her story clears only when held against that of her husband.

Like Olivia, de la Scaze, the Frenchman, has never known love, but also like her he has in his youth made unsatisfying liaisons. Unlike Olivia, however, he has been an artist of sorts. He has written two novels which have had a brilliant success, and he has composed poetry in the years which he thinks of as his "years of secrecy" (418).[4] He discovers, however, quite suddenly, "that his chief emotion in writing a poem" lies "simply, in the fact that he" is "indeed writing a poem" (420). He thinks then of the Mediterranean—that is, of life in some rich sense—and he leaves for Mallorca, there to meet and marry Olivia Barrios. When he discovers that he does not love his beautiful but selfish, "grasping, lascivious, languorous" wife, he feels "a curious sort of relief" (422). He is willing, in other words, at the age of thirty-seven to slip back into his old half-life of dilettantism and enervation. His sojourn in Aqsu reverses this relapse, and his buried instinct for life emerges as an avenger.

As he recuperates from illness, he takes to wandering the streets of Aqsu at night. In the tangled, tempting alleys he is startled by the sight of a beautiful child, a dancing girl. And he hires by accident her brother Hussein as a house boy. To a moderate degree Hussein offers, as does Tansang in Layeville's narrative, an example of wicked but natural behavior. Unlike Layeville, de la Scaze is not disgusted by this Asiatic. On the contrary, his response to Hussein is strongly reminiscent of André Gide's Michel in *The Immoralist*. Michel, it will be remembered, as he recovers from tuberculosis in North Africa, is delighted by the egoistic vitality of the young Moktu who lies and steals. Like Michel, de la Scaze discovers through Hussein that his own life has—during all the years of being repressed—continued, latent and cunning.

But Michel, Gide's immoralist, recovers his life. De la Scaze dies, for Hussein's sister is death. Or so one gathers, for Hussein tells de la Scaze early in the narrative that when cholera comes to the city "all the strangers die" (399). Toward the end of the narrative, when cholera is stalking the streets, Hussein tells him that he need not fear his sister for the reason that she "is never cruel to strangers" (460). Hence, the inadequacies of his early life, his ignorance and rejection of vitality, turn upon him; they become death disguised in the loveliness of apricot-colored flesh. Like Thomas Mann's Aschenbach in "Death in Venice," de la Scaze cannot bring himself to flee the plague, choosing instead to follow the suicidal will-o-the-wisp of a child through a maze of ancient streets.

Although Paul de la Scaze dies of cholera, he does not die without obtaining a certain understanding. He writes down in his diary the "four types of evil." These are:

> First, absence of . . . "good will guided by reason." . . . Men like that Russian Serafimov.
> Second, sterility. This is the sin of acedia, of laziness. An inability to perform good. . . . Layeville.
> Third, triviality. Materialism. . . . Goupillière for example.
> Fourth, demoniac possession. This might be the result of a prolonged accumulation of unexpressed energy; inhibitions; e.g. religious mania. Paranoia (404).

But he appends beneath these categories: "No. Evil is none of these. Evil cannot be explained in terms of human weakness." And a few days later he adds: "Pain sometime brings lucidity but sometimes a sheer elaboration of illusion. We need illusion as we need bread, without it we die. I have learned one thing. As long as I live I shall struggle against seeing things too clearly! My life and eternal happiness depend on the success of this self-conscious deception" (405).

The entries in the diary evoke two comments. First, the reader infers that the title of the novel concerns the seven deadly sins. Yet these sins do not precisely correspond to the medieval catalogue: pride, lechery, envy, anger, covetousness, gluttony, and sloth. And, of course, de la Scaze lists only four "evils," not seven. Second, one assumes that the fourth evil, demoniac possession, resulting from a "prolonged accumulation of unexpressed energy," is de la Scaze's own evil. One knows, too, that his realization that he hides this truth from himself is the beginning of its revelation. And so, as he is dying in the fever of cholera, he believes that the devil talks with him. But this devil is merely his buried self. He wears a blue shirt, and de la Scaze as a child had always pictured Satan as being so dressed. When he leaves, he drops a calling card with "Paul de la Scaze" printed on it. The words of this submerged self in a blue shirt suggest the final knowledge that comes to de la Scaze:

> This matter of evil. Has it ever occurred to you that perhaps we have all been wrong all these years? That perhaps those very things we prefer to hide, whose existence we must arduously strive to forget, called evil . . . perhaps these things called evil, when so enchained in darkness by general consent, so called propriety, gnaw at something in us that is far more important? That is, our soul? Perhaps they should be recognized, released into action, nourished even—(467-68).

To de la Scaze has come a different sense of being, a new self—but no victory.

Now, in what way, is the story of Paul de la Scaze significantly intertwined with Olivia's? Their marriage does bring together two inadequate beings. De la Scaze's life is wasted because, like his poetry, it has ceased to have relevance to the world and has become a form, without gusto or purpose. Olivia's life seems about to be wasted because it is all emotion and has no form, no symmetry at all. These two characters do not affect each other very directly, but they do finally exchange personalities. When Olivia notices the prostitutes in the city of Wanhsien, she sees that they have "groped their way past reality." She longs at this moment "almost to be one of them" (346). In their stylization, their denial of heart and mind, they have become like a lifeless art, or like Paul de la Scaze's poetry. When Olivia accepts a life of prostitution, she is transformed into what de la Scaze had been. One cannot call her change a triumph, any more than one can call his a victory. For Paul in his change becomes what Olivia has been. Significantly, on one occasion when he is asked his name in Aqsu, he says that it is "Barrilot," a slight variation of Olivia's maiden name, "Barrios."

Looking back on these tales, one perceives that *The Seven Who Fled* is an extremely rich allegory. One sees perhaps, first of all, an allegory of Europe before World War II. The stories of Layeville, Serafimov, Wildenbruch, and Von Wald specifically illuminate a national consciousness or character, the dying British Empire, the inarticulate Soviet energy, the ghastly dialogue of fascism in the German soul. The stories of Paul and Olivia de la Scaze and of Goupillière further extend a picture of the Europe dizzy with purposelessness and neurosis.

One is also aware, surely, of the spiritual arguments of these tales. In the conflict of direct opposites, in the disassociation of the "good" Von Wald from the mad Wildenbruch, in the exchange of character between Olivia and Paul de la Scaze, *The Seven Who Fled* tries to face a paramount problem of the modern individual: how to integrate the personality. Prokosch suggests a simple formula over and over again. Cease, he suggests, to believe in good and evil as such. If good and evil exists, they are beyond the comprehension of man. Retain humility and look out from the personality. Recognize the polar aspects of life, learn from one's opposite, but do not seek to destroy that opposite or to fuse with it. One notes, in this respect, that only Joachim Von Wald succeeds in realizing all of these prescriptions. He does so, not merely because of his natural angelism but also because of his intuitive acquiescence in the final and most important allusive symbol in the novel, a symbol which attaches itself to two characters of little importance in the action but which is of grave importance in the meaning of *The Seven Who Fled*. These are Dr. Liu and the Russian Mordovinov who shelters Wildenbruch and Von Wald.

Mordovinov is a saint who has escaped from the world. He sees the modern distresses of materialism, conformity, and boredom; he believes these produce in society a desire for annihilation. As for himself, he says: "The only thing that matters is what you see in my hideous old face, a bit of it still left—the fieriness that should set our lives aflame, even if it plunge us into doom. We should be lifted above our lives, high above the things we see and touch; our spirits should grow intense and passionate. To feel, to endure, to be purified by fire"! (282).

Mordovinov speaks for all the characters in an ideal sense. Even de la Scaze feels himself "purified" in his dying moments. And of course Mordovinov's remote valley represents some halcyon retreat of the spirit. Yet the valley is no absolute triumph over the world, for Mordovinov himself suffers, like de la Scaze and Layeville, from a feeling that he has failed to use a part of his energies. The true wisdom is to be found in Dr. Liu, about whom the reader knows nothing except that Dr. Liu himself knows everything about the others. In the Prologue he asks Layeville why he is in Sinkiang, and he ticks off possible reasons, nodding at the other six Europeans in turn: "Exile? Fear? Exhaustion? Languor? Adventurousness? Ambition?" (12). That is to say, he has in order touched upon the natures of Serafimov, Goupillière, de la Scaze, Olivia, Von Wald, and Wildenbruch. He has also been tactful enough not to mention "sterility" in the presence of Layeville. But he knows about Layeville. Later when Layeville decides to join another caravan in order to reach Tibet, Dr. Liu tells him that he will never reach Shigatse. When he says these words, his eyelids tremble "with a certain malicious pleasure." Layeville thinks that Dr. Liu is either a "very wicked man, or he had ceased to have any feeling at all toward life except one of ironical amusement" (50).

The last one sees of Dr. Liu is in Olivia de la Scaze's story where she, too, feels a similar uncertainty about him. Yet, if she is afraid of him, she also feels when he smiles at her "as if she were waking up" (330). That he is aware of her destiny as of Layeville's is revealed by his insistence that it would be "unwise" (the same word he applies to Layeville's decision to go to Tibet) for her to go to Shanghai. The reason that she feels as if she is awaking is that Dr. Liu personifies in an absolute way the idea of "art"—that very solution which she is seeking, though she selects a dead rather than vital form. Why does Dr. Liu personify art? Partly because he is not malicious *or* ironically detached as Layeville and Olivia feel him to be, but because he is both malicious and detached and because he has brought his own life to a serenity which exceeds Mordovinov's. He says to Olivia, as he shows her an art object: "Such artifice . . . such unreality! Ah, I should like to change into something out of beaten gold, or watered silk, or graven jewels, or procelain, when I die! All things that are truly beautiful, truly serene, are created! Serene and beautiful because nothing can alter them. That is true beauty. The tranquil, the everlasting" (329).

The moment one reads these words he is swept into the cosmogony of William Butler Yeats's poem "Sailing to Byzantium"—not merely because of the ideas but also because of the image of an artifice of beaten gold. Like the bird in Yeats's poem, contrived for the amusement of an emperor, the object contains within itself the essential repose of art. One remembers, too, the beginning of Yeats's poem with its observation, plangent with both decision and despair, that the world of flesh and blood, the world of passion, is no world for an old man. He must seek a citadel of the soul. Dr. Liu's cryptic tolerance, his seeming malice and wisdom do, certainly, stem from his having seen through all passions to the point where he can behold life, concentrated and static, in hard, formal essences. He has moved one step beyond Mordovinov's vision. One is tempted to say of Dr. Liu, in reference to Yeats's poem "Lapis Lazuli," that his eyes are glittering and gay.

Having come this far toward a Yeatsian vision, one might care to wonder if all of the arrangements of self and anti-self in *The Seven Who Fled* do not also pay homage to Yeats's similar view of life. For in *A Vision* (1927) Yeats argued a psychology based on the belief in a primary personality composed of *Will* and of *Mask* (the will's opposite self, which is also the image of what a person desires to become). Significantly, there were for Yeats two masks: one true, one false—and the will is entirely capable of choosing the wrong mask. One wonders if all the characters of *The Seven Who Fled*, with the exception of Von Wald, do not choose an anti-self which in some way is the wrong one: a destructive one. Von Wald avoids a fatal choice among his interior alternatives because he is continuously moving toward art. For, like Dr. Liu, he conceives life in symbols:

> These symbols became real, since life is all in all so intense, he knew, so torrential and moving on the one hand, and on the other so fragmentary and so tormented by unfulfilled dreams, that it can be grasped only through symbols, whatever these may be. Indeed, in what other guise can the desires which govern our lives appear to us, he wondered, than as those shapes which we, in our brief and straying lives, have learned to recognize with our own hearts (312)?

Prokosch's admiration for Yeats is well known, but one cannot brusquely say, nor could Frederic Prokosch, to what degree the interplay of anti-selves derives from Yeats's views. One can, after all, find the views elsewhere—as did Yeats himself. One could even come upon them innocently without guides from another. One can say that the quest for integrity wherein the particles of the soul whirl in a demonic dance led Prokosch to do his best work, *The Seven Who Fled,* and his most recent novel, *The Seven Sisters.*

III   The Seven Sisters

The Seven Sisters (1962) is less directed toward a configuration of anti-selves or the possible emergence of a false, destructive self, than toward the layers of being and the emergence through love of a true self. *The Conspirators* asks, "What idiocy compels man, alone of all creatures, to build walls around his heart?" (32). The question is appropriate to *The Seven Sisters* which among a number of things ponders what happens to love in a world flattened by socialism and technology. To ponder this question is, of course, to be concerned with what happens to the value of intensity in life. To such a point the novel finally moves, but it does so by achievements on dramatic and psychological levels which must be explored before the allegory unfolds.

The title of the novel brings to mind the constellation of *The Pleiades,* as well as the seven deadly sins; but, while the book nods at both allusions, it has no specific involvement in either. It tells the stories of the seven Nightingale sisters, and these all ultimately illuminate one character, an orphan, Peter Kosowsky.

Because of the complex lives of Mr. and Mrs. Nightingale, hardly any of the sisters can claim the same father and mother. Mrs. Nightingale, originally Russian, had been married twice before marrying Mr. Nightingale who had also been previously married. As the novel opens in 1941, Mr. Nightingale has long since given up his career as a diplomat, and the family lives in a decaying ancestral estate at Bishop's Landing on Chesapeake Bay. After World War II ends and after the suicide of Mr. Nightingale, the sisters become separated. One, Elizabeth, dies early. Another, Daphne, who feels no one loves her, runs away. The eldest, Augusta, because she feels unloved and unloving, marries the unprepossessing son of another aristocratic family. When she is able to admit to herself that the marriage is a self-betrayal, she returns to Bishop's Neck where only Grace, the youngest sister, has stayed. The three remaining sisters, along with Peter, go to Europe with Mrs. Nightingale. And these three soon separate from one another. All the stories possess interest; three of them glow with Frederic Prokosch's unique genius for creating a fitful but proud reality from fantastic materials.

Elizabeth's story is short, but it is not without importance in the whole design. Miss Malachi, the girls' sibylline governess, always characterizes Elizabeth as "pure." The characterization is borne out. Elizabeth never self-consciously troubles herself with love as do the others. She innocently loves snakes, which are "dangerous" according to the lascivious Consuelo or "repulsive" according to the repressed Augusta. She sees, in other words, in the snake a beauty which may or may not be phallic but which in either case is not distorted by neurosis. The snake, however, is the god of the underworld; and it is from snake-bite that she dies.

In what way does her little legend relate to the others? In the first place, Elizabeth partakes of certain qualities of each of her sisters: "She was blond like Barbara. She had freckles like Daphne. She loved animals, like Augusta. She had visions like Grace. Like Freya she was perpetually loitering down by the water and like Consuelo she'd go dancing at dusk through the corridors." At the same time that we are given this information, Prokosch informs us that she keeps a collection of dolls: "Russian dolls and Chinese dolls, Haitian puppets and Peruvian marionettes, dolls of wax, dolls of plaster, dolls with patterned chintz bodies, every conceivable kind of doll except those vulgar dolls that looked like babies, all cast in a tangled heap on the studio shelf like a pile of corpses" (34).

The passage yields its meaning gracefully. The dolls, like the dolls which Beatrice Cenci inspects through the haze of her guilt, embody the purity of childhood. That there are no dolls that look like "babies" is significant also of her freedom from sexuality. Because she reflects the traits of her sisters, one way or another, she represents, thus, their innocence which dies with childhood. Her death is, like the tapping of a conductor's baton, a signal for the other stories to begin; for, like all of Prokosch's work, these stories take place in a fallen world.

Augusta, the eldest of the sisters, believes that she loathes men. Indeed, the reader is reminded that, like the goddess Diana, she is a sylvan virgin who is fond of archery. She loves animals, we are told, rather than men. Still, when she rides her gelding, the horse, despite his fondness for her, is always "nervous" (38). If the gelding is aware that Augusta is not at heart a marble virgin, so too is Augusta herself. Hence, as a result of her fearing an absence of love, she marries Cyrus Aspinwall. Her marriage with this crane-like scion of a neighboring family is never consummated. Nevertheless, she eventually realizes that her "feelings of rot and revulsion were really masks which hid the face of a darker and more dangerous emotion" (51). Her revulsion toward sexuality masks her attraction toward it. The revulsion finally alters, and she experiences sexual knowledge with the silenus-figure, Cleophas; and she leaves Cyrus to return to Grace at Bishop's Neck. At a bare psychological level her story is one of repression.

Prokosch associates Augusta closely with Daphne, informing the reader that Augusta has a "shadowy affinity" with Daphne (33). And Augusta, contemplating her loveless state before she decides to marry Cyrus, reflects: "I used to love Daphne but then that ugly thing happened and now there's a wall between Daphne and me" (39). What the ugly thing is we are not precisely told, but we are pretty well forced to conclude that it somehow involves some vague sexual experimentation. This relationship, we think, underlies Daphne's desire to be a boy.

Daphne and Augusta stand in the relation of impetuous nymph to a vestal goddess. Like Augusta, Daphne feels unloved, and, like her, she flees the nest in an attempt to affirm her identity. In her role as a nymph, her career duplicates certain motives in the classic myth of her namesake, Daphne, the daughter of Peneus. Daphne seeks consolation in a tree, which for her is "The Tree," or symbolically the laurel into which the nymph was changed when she fled the amorous advances of Apollo. Ironically, from this very tree she witnesses her mother and Cleophas in the act of love. When her faith in her own Augusta-like virginity is thus challenged, she cuts her hair, dresses as a boy, and leaves Bishop's Neck. The sexual disguise is, of course, the equivalent of changing into a tree in order to escape love. As she roams, she encounters on a river bank a sailor dying from wounds suffered in a fight. He supposes her a homosexual boy, yet speaks to her with affection, so that she feels her female virginity intact while at the same time she feels loved. The effect is that of confirming her in her disguise and making possible her sapphic relationship with Mona. Mona, who is middle aged, stops her car to give Daphne a ride, perceives immediately that she is a girl and takes her to her home on an island off the Florida coast. Of the utmost symbolic import, Daphne changes her name to "Diana" when she joins Mona.

Just as Augusta's detestation of sexuality covers sexual desire, so too does Daphne's Diana disguise. On the island she meets a Cuban boy, Pancho Lopez, who has fled from Brooklyn in fear of civilization and lives on sun (like Apollo), water, and oranges. He has also fled in fear of love. His vocabulary is hardly Apollonian but one interprets his fear of "gang-bangs" and "sexual disease" as a fear of love itself. His distrust of civilization has converted him into a primitive artist. Out of driftwood and pebbles he creates shapes, half animal, half human, which he calls his gods, which "comfort" him "when he is gloomy" (124). When these two fugitives, these two virgins, fall in love, they must again flee, only this time not from love but from the wrath of Mona, who like a moon-hag guards Diana's sanctuary.

In Maine, where Daphne and Pancho go because Pancho has a friend (Jason) there, Daphne gives up her boy-disguise. Ironically, however, Mona's relationship to Daphne is paralleled by Jason's relationship to Pancho. While Daphne is strengthened by being separated from Mona, Pancho is weakened by being associated with Jason. His love for her becomes "alien and scornful" (212). When he dies in a storm, he has already been won by Jason, the sterile artist. But Daphne at least has discovered her essential femininity, so that, when weird Mona comes to Maine to claim her, she can reject Mona and return to Augusta and Grace at Bishop's neck.

As for Grace's story, it is the most tantalizing, at times the most beautiful of the lot, yet ultimately it disappears into an excess of symbol and obscurity. In general we may observe that Grace, unlike the others, never leaves home; she neither runs from love nor after it. She remains instead with Miss

Malachi, trading her own visions for Miss Malachi's Cumean oracles. Lame, lemur-eyed Grace, who is part Negro—the by-blow of one of Mrs. Nightingale's indiscretions—drifts into a world of nightmarish fantasies. She knows that the phantasmagoric creatures she sees are not real, yet they are more real for her than reality. She suggests, then, the soul's capacity to live in the imagination, or to set the imagination between the self and the world. This capacity is not only her power, but also her frailty; for reality takes a strange revenge.

She is haunted by a memory of a rustic boy, Jasper, whom she meets briefly and never sees again. We cannot be absolutely sure that he was ever real, but she feels that he has died, like a lover in a ballad, of unrequited love for her. When she gives her first piano concert, she collapses, thinking she sees in the audience his accusing face. Through a ouija board he tells her what she is to do. The advice is odd, but she follows it. She goes to a house of prostitution, arranges to receive a client, becomes pregnant, and dies in childbirth in the very cave where Jasper had laid down his bones. The novel makes no specific derogation of Grace's rarified activities, nor need one feel that her disappearance into fantasy and symbolism underlies an inability to bring her musical genius to fruition. Though Jasper's spirit voice advises her to act in the physical world, the resulting pregnancy conducts her not to a tragic or to a pointless death but to a "fulfillment" (404)—not, one supposes, because the mind's symbolic faculty cannot withstand reality, but because it must be based on acceptance of reality rather than its rejection.

The remaining sisters, Consuelo, Barbara and Freya, along with Peter, accompany Mrs. Nightingale to Europe. Like those who remain in America, they soon follow different courses.

Consuelo, whose story almost perfectly contrasts with Grace's, studies for a bit at the Sorbonne. She hates stuffiness and thinks, like a number of Prokosch's heroines, of becoming a dancer. Like the dancer-heroines, she is trapped by her own vitality: by her lechery. Consuelo becomes the mistress of a Hungarian refugee whose terrorist activities force them to flee from Paris to Spain and at last to Portugal. Dimitri, like all of Prokosch's conspirators, is deeply divided. He is driven by a political idealism which, as it energizes him, also maims and weakens him. As Consuelo's and Dimitri's sexual relationship intensifies, all their other characteristics deteriorate until life becomes for them as empty and feverish as the utterly introverted lust of the gambler. Whoever believes only in luck, Prokosch suggests, will have none. Consuelo's drowning is not premeditated, but neither is it exactly an accident. The truly dedicated lecher can only seek death.

Barbara's story, while not so original nor so haunting as Daphne's, is the most brilliantly told. Not even Lawrence Durrell is better than Prokosch at pressing scene and mood into such an intense congruency that one never thinks of looking for cleavage lines. And Barbara's narrative brings the reader a Rome and a Venice which may readily be seen as the paintings of a master if one bothers to contrast them with the shockingly dull snapshots offered by a good deal of recent fiction.

The most beautiful of the sisters, blonde Barbara, uses her loveliness to gain power. She says, "All my life has been tainted with this horrible fear of failure. . . . I made a vow. To be rich. To be calculating and ruthless" (89). Hence, when wealthy, aging Prince Massimo offers her marriage, she listens with wicked ears attuned to "the pulse of destiny" (79) and accepts. Yet her wealth and power bring her no happiness, for she cannot give herself, either to the weary prince or to his nephew Alessandro with whom she becomes infatuated. She assumes always that she must use people and that to do so she must reserve herself from them. The curious result of her passion for power over people is that she does not at all know what they are like. She considers Alessandro—as beautiful and as ambivalent as the Antinous in the Vatican—to be only a means of delighting her flesh. When, however, in his studio she inadvertently sees the photographs he has taken, she turns in dismay from this revelation of his personality which she has helped to create.[5] Furthermore, all the while that she deliberately deceives herself about others, guilt grows within her; lust, tyranny and hollowness show in her face. Alessandro escapes from her, and the prince— to whom it is hinted she gives the wrong medicine—dies. With Mrs. Nightingale she leaves Rome for Venice.

In Venice, one evening in a shabby quarter of the city, she becomes lost and hysterical. Then she is confronted by a projection of her guilt, a meretricious and vulgar gallant, who tells her that she has "rejected the terrors of real experience," preferring "other terrors, the subtler and more insidious terrors." These, he adds are: "The terrors of living in a perpetual self-deluding limbo. Not out of ignorance. Nor even hard luck. . . . Not out of timidity even. . . . But out of vanity. . . . What might have been remorse, what might have been a struggle of conscience or even a genuine reaching of a soul—you finally reduced it all to petulance. *Superbia et vanitas!*" (346). At this point Barbara changes. She enters a church and, asking forgiveness for her "vanity" and "pride," she prays to be made "human" and "real" again (350). The thematic implication of the tale does not require further comment.

In the Epilogue to *The Seven Sisters* Peter says that "Maybe it was love that Freya was pursuing and maybe it was love that Barbara was fleeing." Augusta answers, "And then everything was turned around. They exchanged their roles" (403). Freya does, like Barbara, reverse the direction of her life. She early seeks—in her painting and in her restive love of islands—to remain free or "to reduce the chaos into dimensions that she [can] handle" (391). In Capri or Sicily, if love is offered, she gathers up her easel and seeks another island. Ironically, on an Aegean Island, as she is about to run from blind Demetrius, his wife accosts her, mutilating her face. Freya then decides that she wishes to change herself. She becomes "horrified" by islands and by her paintings. Like Julia in T. S. Eliot's *The Cocktail Party,* she becomes a saint, dying as a social worker in a village in a Brazilian jungle.

In Freya's conversion to selflessness we are given a key to the other stories. Though words like "vanity," "sloth" and "lechery" appear in *The Seven Sisters,* the only real sin is self-consciousness—as it is, of course, in patristic theology or in the allegorical schemes of Nathaniel Hawthorne and Herman Melville. On each of the sisters, except Grace and Elizabeth, the brand of egotism burns; and the search for love or the attempt to avoid love derives from an illusion that they are finding "freedom." Even so, their frantic struggles only more surely entangle them, like fish, in a net. Augusta, Daphne, Barbara, and Freya eventually rectify their courses. And even Consuelo appears to change in the dark sea that sucks her out from the shore to her death. She feels emancipated from human error; she feels harmony which life itself never gave to her. We are brought finally to see that, through "befouling" their flesh, five of the sisters "cleansed" their hearts (403). Or, to put it a different way, they at long last compose their lives, discover integrity, and find freedom. And yet the ultimate effect of the allegory comes to rest with the character of Peter Kosowsky rather than that of the sisters. In a curious tangential way the ultimate effect also involves the shadowy hunter, Cleophas.

Peter and Cleophas have in common their yearning to belong to the seven sisters. At a literal level, Cleophas' yearning stems from his awareness that he is their half-brother; at a symbolic level, Cleophas represents instinct and nature. He is a hunter. He kills without cruelty and without remorse. He copulates at random with no sense of sin. He invites Peter as a child to witness his fleshly pleasures. Whatever happens, he considers "natural"— not good, not bad. His longing, then, to unite with the Nightingale sisters (a little like Apeneck Sweeney among the nightingales) implies the reluctance of nature to relinquish man to civilization. It also implies the reverse: the reluctance of man to abandon nature as he careers toward a destiny which takes him far from his origins. Cleophas is reminiscent of Matthew Arnold's forsaken merman who calls to his human wife to return to the sea.[6]

Peter himself is both drawn toward Cleophas and disgusted by him. His disgust arises from the very naturalness which he adores. In the most extended symbolic sense, Cleophas represents the amoral basis of life: the natural self which one must both respect and transcend. Hence, though Augusta feels disgust for him, she comes to realize that the disgust masks sexual desire. When she couples with Cleophas, she can construct a truce among the warring forces of her being. Similarly Elizabeth, the innocent, *merely* loves snakes: there exists no need for her, then, to come to terms with a sexual side of her nature. Grace "accepts" a phallic law in the universe. So, also, does Peter, but it must equally be realized that Peter views the sisters not only in relation to Cleophas but also in relation to himself.

For these sisters portray, in a final sense and in contrast to Cleophas, the anti-natural or spiritual possibilities of life and specifically that within Peter himself. Such is the implication in his words to Augusta at the end of the novel: "Do you know what Grace said to me? She said that all seven of you were really the same person. And that what happened to one of you really happened to all seven of you, and so in the end you shared in the same experiences" (403).

One can go so far as to say that the seven sisters present to Peter seven faculties in a constellation. These faculties include Elizabeth's complete but nevertheless always lost innocence, as well as Grace's ability to order and hence accept phenomena through the symbolic imagination. The others offer possibilities in attitude either for good or bad behavior, for fulfillment or for frustration, for wholeness or fracturing of the sensibilities; possibilities for sins of pride, sloth, vanity or for virtues of humility, industry and discovery; possibilities for a destructive war with Cleophas, which he will always win, or a constructive peace. But one must go a step further and ponder why Prokosch places Peter, who at first sight seems characterless, in conjunction with the dynamic sisters.

Like all of Frederic Prokosch's heroes, Peter is carefully orphanized, isolated, cut adrift and alone. He lives at the beginning of the novel with his aged grandmother; but she, though she seems as eternal as the earthmother, soon dies. He spends a short time at an orphanage, but, even here, his one friend is drowned. The reasons for Prokosch's preferring an orphanic hero are multiple and intricate, and one would be on boggy ground should he attempt to discover all of them. Of clear importance, however, is the fact that a certain isolation not only characterizes the artist but also is necessary to him. Peter Kosowsky is an artist, a painter.

Despite his modest protestations of incompetence, Peter is dedicated to art; despite the mask of guilelessness, one must see that he is groping toward understanding. His reactions to the paintings of the masters in the Louvre are worthy to stand with André Malraux's art criticism. One example is sufficient. Of de la Tour's *Saint Joseph Charpentier*, he observes:

The light of the candle shone through the hand of the watching child, transforming the upheld fingers into a luminous rosy parchment, and it fell on the wrinkled brow of the sad old carpenter, which said all worth saying about goodness and endurance. It was a scene of a barren and somber simplicity but it burst into flame from the sense of wonder that hung over it, so that the flame of the candle looked like a soaring exclamation point shining on the whole impenetrable mystery of human existence (161).

This is not the reaction of one who is insipid or inexperienced. But then, Peter is neither. The seven sisters, along with Cleophas, are, objectively, his life. What eventually the seven stories mean is the meaning of his life, his discovery. He must learn, of course, in what way, from his lonely prospect, he can form a relationship with the world. In an Italian hill village he thinks as follows:

He had always felt as though he were dangling. He had never gotten a foothold. . . . He felt nowhere that he was a part of things; he felt nowhere that he belonged. . . . And the only answer he could imagine to all this dangling and rootlessness was to become a member of the entire world, the human world that had no boundaries, the world of humanity regardless of place or of background. But just how to achieve this membership was difficult to imagine, and the only way seemed to be by attaining a kind of inner purity, by painting without prejudice and thinking without prejudice and by loving everything equally, irrespective of place or background (154-55).

His loneliness and his desire for a focus or "home" drive him to seek his family in Poland. He finds neither home nor an end to loneliness with his grandfather and stepsister. But he finds that loneliness and homelessness are his own destiny, that they are "a mask for something else, an elaborate camouflage for a deeper intensity" (381). That "deeper intensity" is the dedication and responsibility of the artist. The realization of his destiny is the true beginning of his life and of his understanding of his relationships with the seven sisters of his interior being and with the magnet of nature: Cleophas. Even more, these relationships give way to a relationship at once objective and subjective with humanity. Or, so one sees if one correctly interprets his journey into the Brazilian jungle to find Freya, to find "freedom," a freedom born of sacrificing oneself to humanity. For in his relationship with the native boy Aipuri, Peter comes to terms with humanity, or at least with the symbol of it. There is no intellectual meeting between him and the ignorant primitive, but there is interdependence, a mutual recognition of the long, absurd history of mankind; and there is love—cool, somewhat amused and ironical, but true.

In a word, the artist has found maturity. That maturity is the central theme of *The Seven Sisters* is evident from the strange old fairy tale the grandmother tells Peter as a child. She tells of finding as a girl in Poland a tiny woodsprite who cries out for help and implores her to grieve for him, for he is bewitched. When she weeps for him, the sprite grows into a child, then a boy, then a youth, and finally ages and dies. The grandmother draws the moral that "it's better to crumble and die than never grow up at all. And it's only through pity and love that people grow up" (6). When Peter goes to Poland, his half-sister tells him a similar story of a frog that asks her to weep for him. She weeps, and the frog becomes a young man whom she says looked like Peter. She cannot remember what happened after, but the reader can remember the grandmother's story and add that the acceptance of death is a part of maturity.

The Seven Sisters is, along with *The Seven Who Fled*, among Frederic Prokosch's finest achievements. It brings into definition all the problems less certainly resolved in his earlier volumes. Furthermore, it allows the reader finally to see what his real contribution to the literature of this century has been. His contribution has not been, one sees now, to participate like Hemingway in the public experience of his generation; it has been to participate in the psychic experience of his generation. He has not marched on the broad plain. He has wandered in a narrow chasm, fitfully lit, haunted by phantoms and echoing with the voices of dangerous memories. One would be foolish to take his chasm as the whole truth; but it would be equally foolish to take as the whole truth the armies marching on the plain.

CHAPTER 7

The Novels: A Critical Conclusion

I *Theme*

AT THE HEIGHT of his popularity, Frederic Prokosch wrote of his literary aims:

> What I have humbly tried to do is to move a step closer to the literature of the future—which will, I feel sure, like life itself pass gradually beyond national limitations; I have tried to bring the American point of view and the European into an imaginative harmony; to sail between those deadly twins, commercialism and clique; to detect a universal and lasting pattern in each contemporary situation; to humanize intellect with feeling, and invigorate feeling with intellect; to attain a style which will neither falsify nor deaden, but at all times illuminate; and above all, never to forget that man is now as always a terrifying animal who can be clearly perceived only through the cooperating powers of compassion, fearlessness, and love.[1]

This clear statement calls for no elucidation; but, since it circumscribes the territory of much of Prokosch's work, it also sets the ground rules for any critical evaluation of the total accomplishment.

Prokosch is not alone, of course, in his depiction of the flavor of internationalism in his novels and poetry, but his contribution to the genre is unique. He is not so concerned as was Henry James with the contrast of cultures brought into confrontation. Nor is he so concerned with the comparison of cultures as is Lawrence Durrell. Prokosch is not primarily interested in the exilic or expatriate viewpoint which fascinated Hemingway and many others in this century. Prokosch's interest and concern, while partaking of cultural contrast and comparison, largely re-

flect a vogue, almost a mystical haloing, of the idea of internationalism. This vogue represents a condemnation, really, of
American isolationism prior to World War II. Prokosch's intensity
of conviction could come, really, only to an American, one
supposes, and only to one whose background contained elements
both of provincialism and cosmopolitanism. Only one who was
born early in the twentieth century and whose youth was spent
in Wisconsin, Texas, and European schools would so single-
heartedly desire to collate disparate cultural elements. The word
here is "collate," for there is never any impression that Prokosch
wants to fuse the elements. His Asians do not change his Europeans; his Europeans do not blend with his Americans. However,
when his Americans or Europeans are not destroyed by their
contacts with each other—or, more particularly, by their contacts
with Asians or Africans—they may enrich their lives through
broadening their understanding of themselves.

The attraction of the internationalist novel is simultaneously
personal and intellectually historical. One perceives in Prokosch's
total attitude what one perceives in the attitudes of others of
his generation: the desire to move away from a pessimism and
fatalism implicit in the work of James Joyce, William Butler
Yeats, T. S. Eliot, and Robinson Jeffers and to move with
tentative optimism toward the future. The optimism, not very
noticeable until after World War II, is limited. All the same, the
very idea of internationalism visible even in *The Asiatics*, is
optimistic; for insofar as it substitutes "man" for nationalistic
cultures, it tends to refute Oswald Spengler's obstinate fatalisms
about culture cycles. (Spengler is, after all, the Byron, the dark
Satanic hero, of the twentieth-century mind.) In an extended
way, this substitution and this refutation abide at the heart of
Prokosch's whole thematic structure, even though the earliest
poetry and novels are Spenglerian in their emotions, and knee
deep in the morass of historical doubt. The refutation of cultural
doom rests upon one foundation, that of substituting man as a
genus for man as a culture; but the structure which rises from
this foundation has the intent of bringing man into relation with
history, with nature and with himself.

One cannot avoid the impression that Prokosch's novels rather
fretfully deplore the changes wrought, and about to be wrought,

by the twentieth century. Again and again his earlier novels remind us that the old Europe is dying. His later novels remind us that some change, not so great as had earlier been anticipated, has already taken place and that the future is that of an antiseptic, dull civilization. Yet what is it in the old Europe, that Prokosch so reluctantly gives up? It is not the Europe of 1910 or of the nineteenth century; it is the Europe of the Age of Reason. It is a western civilization incidentally aristocratic but naturally international and one which took man rather than five-year plans as the measure of all things. In reality, Prokosch laments the passage of an era which never in a personal way existed for him and which, indeed, had been swept away by the century preceding his birth.

This lament for the past may be pointless; but, from one's increasingly distant perspective today, it is hard to disagree with Prokosch on this score. We have begun to quarrel less with the seemingly smug moralism of the nineteenth century as we see its hidden truth, the subcutaneous horror of its destructive neurosis and at times of its insanity. But nobody thinks the eighteenth century can be restored. Nor does Frederic Prokosch, but his novels attempt to curb the still continuing momentum of nineteenth-century enthusiasm, and to lead us into a wiser future.

It is noteworthy that Prokosch, who began to write in a decade gravid with political theory and political aesthetics, never endorsed any of the popular stands. He was never a Marxist, he was not a fascist; he was not a liberal. He was wise enough to see that fascism was a disease able to invade only a decadent body politic already weakened by other diseases, but he did not, as did a whole generation of intellectuals, see Marxism as an answer. He saw Marxism as a delusion, or maybe once again, as just another disease. Does all this mean he entertained no beliefs himself? Not exactly, but his belief was entirely concentrated in such a way as to exempt man from political abstractions and from ideals. In *The Skies of Europe,* he ponders the plight of the Marxist and the liberal:

> Why is it? These idealists who invoke a justification of every instinct, who analyze every motive, and pass for men eminently governed by their intellect—these, oddly enough, are precisely

the ones most tyrannized by their own singular emotions . . . I thought of those simple, humble souls that I had seen in every country and every town, men who never dream of invoking their ideals or their intellect and with every appearance of following merely the animal impulses: yet, men invariably guided by a core of common sense, by a delicately balanced humor, by a shrewd and essential grasp of life, its color, its texture, its rhythm . . . While, alas, the self-styled idealist . . . lapses only too swiftly into the limbo of abstractions . . . for what, in effect is wrong with these men is not their veneration of ideas, but the weak and fragmentary nature of their spirit which freezes and categorizes these ideas, isolates them from human activity, and drains them of human blood: so that they grow, with the passing years as hollow and brittle as an eggshell dropped from a nest (144).

This attitude is not anti-intellectual; but it does insist that life is more important than theories about life, that man is more important than history, that humanity is more important than a particular politics or a particular culture. Life, then, for Frederic Prokosch is the only *pragma*; it is the only fact; and such a conception requires that this esteem for the conditions that surround life be pragmatical. He will, in other words, admire those conditions which permit life to realize itself and denigrate those that do not. Therefore, one value particularly recommends itself to him—freedom. But he would not claim that it is inevitably attached to one institution, to one political ideal. He would no doubt say that freedom is incompatible with certain institutions. He certainly says that freedom is incompatible with the state of being a conspirator, even though the conspiracy is directed against tyranny. Life has a duty, according to Prokosch, transcending "isms" and national boundaries; for these are the tyrants of the soul and oppressors of the heart. Life must seek itself in itself.

If the intent of Prokosch's internationalism is to turn life toward life, so also has his faith in freedom a similar aim: to allow the soul scope to pursue its own tragedy. Prokosch uses the word "tragedy" with a romantic largeness. He associates it with "dignity." To a degree, at least, tragedy must mean to him the weaving of individual destiny that is apparent in all of his novels. Prokosch examines both life and its destiny in two different ways. He holds western, civilized men up to the cruel, frank light of Asia, Africa, Brazil. He places them in wastelands and among primitives whose incomprehension finally begets ironic comprehension. Or, he scrutinizes his Europeans and Americans in their great cities: Paris, Rome, New York. The cities function for Prokosch somewhat as do his deserts and jungles, for they extract as well as affect the spirits of his characters. At the same time, the city is clothed in its civilization, while the desert or jungle is nude. The city thus murmurs of the heights of civilization, perhaps passed, perhaps to come, but always with a gentle insistence on the virtues of decorum and intelligence. The glittering badlands of *The Asiatics* or of *Nine Day to Mukalla* bring to the characters a confrontation with instinct and with the other timeless entities of primitives which anthropology has made, with its explanations and analysis, all the more mysterious. Unquestionably, Prokosch longs to coordinate instinct and civilized intelligence, but he does not wish to do so through any romantic dependence on nature.

Man and nature—the world of being as against the world of phenomena—pursue mutually exclusive aims in the work of Frederic Prokosch. Civilized man may appear to be a part of nature when he blends momentarily into its beautiful drift. And he owes his being to nature. But he has gotten in certain ways outside it. His ethics quarrel with the survival of the fittest. His art quarrels with the laws of symmetry. His love neither so fiercely preserves nor so coldly squanders as does nature. In a final sense, nature for Prokosch presents an almost irrelevant beauty. He records it often enough with care and sensitivity. Butterflies and moths punctuate the air; the feel of water, the texture of obsidian, the myriads of reptiles and beasts—all these haunt the novels. But all of these go their own way, not the way of human life. Nature, for all its elegance, is, for Prokosch, an idiot. Nature is the past with which modern man seeks an accommodation, but into which he must not retrogress. Indeed, to do so, would be to abandon his freedom and to deny his destiny both as an individual and as a species. To sink back into nature would be to surrender to a mindlessness where tragedy cannot exist.

For Prokosch does not imbue nature, as did Wordsworth, with goodness or, as did Shelley, with intelligence. Though he is amazed at its energy and though he respects its law, he does not worship nature. Not only does he refuse to worship nature: he rejects it ultimately in favor of a triangulation of a mystical sense of history, individual development, and the ineluctable framework of fable or legend. To understand what he does with character, one must continuously remember that legend or myth along with a Germanic view of history form the other two sides of the triangle.

II *Character*

Frederic Prokosch creates character within a severely restricted range beyond which he cannot, or will not, go. We may easily catalogue the categories: the faceless hero, the sly but engaging aborigine, the promiscuous and ambitious heroine, the "tragic" artist, the conspirator, the homosexual, the European or American whose sensibilities are whipped into hysteria by exposure to a circumstance or to a savage setting. In addition, the novels are salted with creatures, *creatures* rather than characters, who appear briefly to present a tantalizing surface of inscrutable gesture but who disappear like figures in a nightmare without any sure resolution.

The faceless hero derives from both subjective and objective elements. The suspicious reader will be fully aware that this hero is never so characterless, so sexless, and so insipid as the surface of the novels imply. But Prokosch prefers to have the reader establish his hero's experience on the basis of the activities of other characters; for, as in *The Seven Sisters*, one must piece together Peter's awareness from that of all the Nightingale sisters. The disadvantage of such an approach is that one feels the author is less interested in revealing a character than in protecting him. One gets tired of guessing and—quite unfairly—decides that Prokosch is really protecting himself. Even our understanding of the evolution of this hero may not lead to forgiveness. However, Prokosch's distrust and, at times, his contempt for abstract solutions to life and politics force him to create a hero who possesses few if any convictions of the kind which recommend themselves to the ordinary moral or practical hopes of mankind. He feels committed neither to a Victorian view of sexual behavior nor to a modern latitudinarian view. He deplores political tyranny but he does not uphold democracy or, indeed, any other system as such. And so his hero's want of positive belief may seem a strange feebleness, or, if not that, a sinister tolerance. All the same, his hero's quality of being disengaged often contrasts effectively with the absurd engagement of many of the other characters who constantly embrace extremes which contradict and eventually tend to cancel each other. In his most successful work, the extreme views erode away, leaving the implication that the hero's neutrality is in reality an alliance with essentials of greater import than fashionable views.

The anonymous hero is connected also with Prokosch's allegiance to internationalism. If he disapproves of national boundaries, then Prokosch must also disapprove of national faith and theory. His hero may not, therefore, make choices or state beliefs that in themselves are confined to nations or to particular political cults. Thus, his heroes are always shown to be men without countries—either by choice, as they wander in the world, or by accident, as they sojourn in self-imposed exile. A curious irony develops from all this. The man without a country, or without a civil commitment, suggests himself as hero to Prokosch because he desires to emphasize a quality of life that transcends nation and "ism." Yet for that very reason, his hero himself may lack certain qualities of life. In his dedication to humanity, be becomes inhuman. In his faith in vitality, he becomes devitalized.

This limitation of concept gives rise to serious critical strictures on the work of Frederic Prokosch. Nor is there any dismissing the problem. In fact, the problem is compounded by the other characters, at least by those who are civilized. So many of the characters seem specimens preserved in a museum. Particularly do the fatal, lascivious women seem always to be creeping toward their niches in the gallery. The more restless they are, the more static they seem. Yet in this examination, hard-hearted but necessary, it would be unfair to lose sight of the fact that these characters are deployed for certain rather odd Pyrrhic victories; it would be equally unfair to ignore that they exist in an aesthetic relationship with other characters.

A frequent observation of reviewers has been that Prokosch's "native" characters seem much more lifelike than his Europeans. The observation is more or less valid, but it requires some further consideration. In the first place, no claim can be made that they are realistic portrayals of Asians, Bedouins, or Africans. Few critics would be in a position to judge! So the whole question comes down to their seeming to be lifelike, of their satisfying some preconception of what extra-European aborigines ought to be rather than what they are. As it happens, Prokosch gives to his Asians, his Africans, and his South Americans identical characteristics: They combine ready affection with slyness and treachery; primitive beauty with colossal vanity; and a dark, superstitious ignorance with some show of intuitive wisdom. When one critically inspects this formula, he becomes, or ought to become, reluctant to insist that these qualities are true of any particular tribe, let alone all the tribes of the Congo or of the Amazon. And very unlikely that they are true of all non-Europeans everywhere in the world. But these qualities are, of course, the very ones which modern man somewhat sentimentally would like to think exist in life somewhere, somehow. These qualities are not exactly heroic virtues, but they impute daring, inscrutability, self-reliance and hence excitement to life—all the things which our civilized hearts yearn for. One does not condemn Prokosch here for being less than scientific; one congratulates him upon creating an artistic anthropology.

One can go further. These "natives" are, in their aesthetic conception, types to whom the most minor peculiarities are given, whose formula is only slightly varied. They are types in the same way that characters in eighteenth-century fiction are types: Their components appeal to assumptions about life rather than to life itself. They contrast, moreover, very tidily with the Europeans who seem idiosyncratics. Strangely enough, the idiosyncratics who can achieve little generality are offered as general symbols while the natives—the type characters—seem individuals. Perhaps this interchange of their aesthetic natures comes from the fact that the civilized characters cannot be natural, while the uncivilized ones cannot but seem natural. However this may be, one must admit that only a talent of an unusual order could so manipulate his characters that they break with probabilities and heretically create an original dimension in fiction.

Types or individuals, most of Prokosch's characters pose an unusual problem in motivation. Within the confines of strict psychological realism, one cannot very often assign reasons for the particular behavior of this or that character. One can say that Serafimov is "driven" to murder Goupillière; but one cannot —except on a philosophic basis—say why he was driven. One can say that Tony in *A Ballad of Love* is impelled toward disaster, but one cannot say by what he is impelled. There is a reason in Prokosch's view of his art to account for all this hidden motivation. Once again the reason involves a departure from normal procedures. He writes of his own work:

> I might stress, in general, that I feel isolated from other American writers, poets as well as novelists—my whole approach is so different. Durrell and Nabokov are the only novelists with whom I feel an instinctive affinity these days. My novels are (I suppose) allegorical, mythic, non-realistic, and float in a kind of ultra-national atmosphere of their own—the good ones, anyway.[2]

The fact is that Prokosch writes what Hawthorne in the nineteenth century called "romance"; that is, an allegory in which the real or surface occurrences may much of the time appear illusory, so that only meaning or theme obtains a solidity. In addition to this general aim of romance, Prokosch also writes in the tradition of legend or fable. In these words "legends" and "fable," we come to the nub of the matter. In *The Seven Who Fled* Layeville asks one of the men in the caravan why Salik had murdered three men. "For money?" he wonders. His companion appears not to understand his question. "Why? Because he is a murderer! That is the reason. A murderer . . . not a robber" (37).

We note that the reason for Salik's behavior is not psychological but what Herman Melville would call "a depravity according to nature." It is the nature of Salik to murder. What is true of Salik's motivation is true of the motivation in varying degrees of all of Prokosch's characters—just as, in the final analysis, it is true of that in all of Hawthorne's characters. It is a waste of breath to ask ordinary motivation from Prokosch, just as it would be a waste of breath to ask Aesop why his fox is cunning. By nature the fox is cunning. Now, motivation, as it is practiced in the twentieth-century novel is simply a matter of showing why a character behaves *contrary to his nature.* The assumption is, for example, that character "X" by nature should have been a normal, dull, good citizen. But, his mother has been overly protective; and, as a result, he is not normal, dull, and good; he is abnormal, exciting, and wicked. There is much to be said for Aesop's simple economy.

To see Prokosch's characters as mythic natures is to bring a substantial sympathy not merely to their behavior but also to their manner of speaking. Prokosch has not much talent for dialogue of a realistic sort. When in *Night of the Poor* he attempts to duplicate folk rhythms and dialect, the effect is often painfully embarrassing. To his credit, he seldom attempts anything of the sort. On the contrary, the dialogue is usually highly formal and even ritualistic. The formality has, of course, frequently been condemned as being stilted and unnatural. And so it would be if his novels were realistic. But the intent of his novels is not realism, and the effect of his dialogue is appropriate to the whole atmosphere of legend, which in its purest form demands pure language. We should be disturbed to find Lewis Carroll's Alice speaking like a delinquent who has run away from home. Perseus must speak in a way sufficiently above common speech so as to preserve his idea—indeed, his ideality. Within the framework of these standards, Prokosch's characters must speak so that the gods can understand them. They speak also in such a way as to reveal their natures to mortals. The revelation may be direct or it may be indirect, for they may speak through a disguise or some unconscious covering of the true nature.

Because Prokosch apparently believes faithfully that man is born with a sacred nature, his whole concept of character is that of encouraging that nature to fulfill itself or, if need be, to cast off the disguise created by the fearful self or imposed by modern life. For this reason Prokosch tends to arrange his novels about a general craving for self-awareness. The characters in the early work *The Seven Who Fled* find an occult self rising from a hiding place, but it is a self-destructive self. In the later novels, *A Ballad of Love* and *The Seven Sisters,* there are hints that more than one identity lies obscured in the depths and that to find one self suggests that yet another and perhaps truer self lies below that one. For Henry in *A Ballad of Love,* below the self which is "sensible" and "innocuous" on the surface, lies "a second, more secluded self: sly, patient and calculating, anxious to please but thoroughly unscrupulous, inquisitive and touchy, tenacious and vain. . . . And somewhere in the depths beneath this feline second self, lay coiled a dark and passionate and unpredictable third identity, waiting for its moment to leap forth and commit some wild, irrevocable folly. This was the self that lay hidden, that spoke in a whisper. This was the self that was capable of obsession; that baffled and tormented me. This was the self that under it all gave its mystery to existence; its savagery, its sadness, its touch of the miraculous" (86).

Prokosch is speaking, of course, of what Carl Jung calls the *anima* in the layers of personality; but the importance of the passage is not its intellectual origin. The seemingly flaccid hero of Prokosch's novels derives from the fact that Prokosch chooses to reveal primarily the innocuous surface. Yet the whole truth is that, through other characters and cryptic clues, the submerged selves of his heroes are subtly suggested. They possess a strata of unscrupulous self-serving egotism and beneath that a strata of obsession. The imaginative reader will see that Prokosch's heroes are placed in a basic relationship with beautiful, lustful women, with virile and loving primitives, and (usually but not always) with decadent homosexuals. The final effect is always that of rejecting the decadent homosexual in favor of composing what one might call the true male and female elements of the soul.

Although the philosophic psychology of Carl Jung springs to mind when one contemplates the stratification of these personalities, a possibly better way of probing them reposes in a longer, more historical view. With the concentration upon self in the first impulses of nineteenth-century feeling, one finds the emergence of alter-egos in literature. Presumably for Shelley in *Prometheus Unbound* and for Byron in *Manfred* the simple egoism of Wordsworth was not enough. They accepted the dictum of self, but fractured the self into turbulences of opposition. So it is also, of course, to the extreme in all of the work of Edgar Allan Poe who in "Ulalume" talks with Psyche, his "soul." So also for Stéphane Mallarmé who in his poem "Sigh" speaks of his soul as his "sister." Prokosch, along with other twentieth-century writers, such as Kafka, has multiplied the fracturing of self that is implicit in romantic thought. Modern psychology protects such views, yet one's acceptance of them in literature depends as much upon aesthetic arrangements as it does upon their validity.

III *Style*

Frederic Prokosch's luxuriant prose style is characterized at its most elementary level by a contest between large terms, vague but suggestive, and sharp, brilliant metaphors. He hangs a very great deal—too much, one says finally—on such words as "prehistory," "primitive," and "tragedy." Such abstractions suggest an attempt to shove a number of indefinite emotions into one container in the hope that the container itself will be imposing enough to scare away questions. The terms are a literary equivalent of political jargon, a kind of jingoism of the soul. The term "tragedy," struck so as to set echoing a state of feeling, was employed a good deal in the literature of the 1920's and 1930's. The categorical use derives originally from Nietzsche but directly from Oswald Spengler. One cannot flatly object to the use of such terms of convenience; for, after all, they are found in all literature. But the kind of usage one encounters in Prokosch is suspicious, for the usage is not straightforward. "Tragedy," for example, comes to suggest, among a lot of other things, something like "a painfully beautiful fulfillment approved of by intuition."

Prokosch's metaphors are a different matter, and his talent for analogy is remarkable. Indeed, so prodigal is his talent that he ought to be stern with it and control it. For it does upon occasion run to excess; it does sometimes seem too easy, if only for the reason that it is easy for *him*. Yet when one encounters, for example, in *The Skies of Europe* the following comparison, "Grayhounds, thin and iridescent as almond twigs, lay sleeping in the middle of the dusty street" (217), he knows that he is in the company of a superlative observer. He knows, too, that for Frederic Prokosch details exist in a special relationship to each other; they mirror and marry each other in his mind. Perhaps for the very reason that analogies suggest themselves so readily to him, he is sometimes curiously careless about details. As an illustration, in the opening of *The Seven Sisters,* when Prokosch observes that "the musk of rotting woods and the coppery rush of the pheasant . . . haunt the Chesapeake . . . just as they haunted it a hundred or a thousand years ago," the reader is perturbed by the knowledge that pheasants were introduced into this country from Asia less than a hundred years ago. However, this kind of blemish is rare; and, in general, both the bright details and the fine sense of analogy operate honorably. And, even when there is a flagging, one feels that Prokosch is nevertheless trying to make every sentence hit and that he has faith in the reader's intelligence and sensitivity. And certainly the rich interweaving of metaphor and detail permit Prokosch to create those animated landscapes which are the triumph of his style.

The landscapes, the city scenes, the sense of place can be savored again and again in the novels; but their unique effect does not yield easily to analysis or to description. *Age of Thunder,* one of the least successful of the novels, contains some of Prokosch's finest passages. At one point two artists discuss the light of various countries, finishing up in this way:

> "Yes, and the Italian light is a little hard too but full of a certain resilience and glamour. The sunlight trembles on the leaves in Tuscany and casts hot grape-colored shadows, and all the time I was there I thought of human beings perpetually living and dying. Human nature itself seems to quiver on the rays of sunlight in Italy." Then he paused and said to Amedée, rather humbly: "And Greece? You've been in Greece?"
>
> "Greece," replied Amedée, "has become a dream and that is all. Greece is beyond good and evil and the sunlight in Greece, Ulysse, is the arid, depopulated sunlight of eternity" (61-62).

What happens in these observations? How does Prokosch manage to say more, for example, about the light of Greece than all the writers of travel books put together? The essential element here is that the light functions as a metaphor for both historical and personal emotions. He writes in *The Seven Who Fled* that "landscape is a state of the spirit, it is a constant longing for what is to come, it is a reflection incomparably detailed and ingenious of what is everlasting in us, and everlastingly changing" (300). The words reveal some of the secret: his descriptions are an animation, a sublimation of self and a projection of man's destiny. As such, these landscapes preserve somewhat ironically an inhuman assonance which by contrast underlines the dissonance of human behavior.

A macrocosmic metaphor is not all that informs Frederic Prokosch's spiritual geography. Another quality surrounds the alarming vividness of his pictures. One is tempted to think this quality to be like the storm-light intensity of dreams. It is like that, partly, but only in the sense that dreams take on the aura of memory and, if we allow ourselves a romantic moment, the aura of "ancestral memories"—a phrase and concept for which Prokosch entertains a fondness. In *The Skies of Europe,* he writes:

> When I first set foot in Austria as a boy of five, I was convinced that I had been there before, long ago. And years later, when I . . . sauntered down the darkening streets of Innsbruck, the familiar fragrance of bituminous coal and moldly cellars, the ripples of snow, the clear Tyrolean voices, the lettering over the shops and the shadow of the mountains, all filled me with an exact and burning recognition: for a moment it seemed that all the intervening years had been years of insecurity and exile: that at last I was returning to the warm, kindly home of my peasant and soldier grandfathers (316-17).

His landscapes do indeed contain "an exact and burning recognition" which only the ministration of memory, simplifying and strengthening the outlines, can give. The desert in *Nine Days to Mukalla* or the Tibetan ice-meadows in *The Seven Who Fled* create the peculiar suspension, pose, and intensity of Henri Rousseau's paintings, particularly *The Sleeping Gypsy.* So much does the reader feel that he himself is creating as in a dream or memory some of Prokosch's landscapes that he thinks that, if he were to shut his eyes and open them again, something in the delicate dimension of their temporal span would be lost, and the picture would be gone.

IV *Structure*

Most critics have granted the power of Prokosch's landscapes, but most have scorned the organization of his novels. If one is looking for tidy outlines and Swiss movement, all one can do is scorn. But, in failing to find a conventional success, the critic fails to discover the actual success: Prokosch is a master of form —not of the novel, but of the novelette. *The Seven Who Fled* is a collection, really, of short novels. And, if one were to rearrange *The Seven Sisters* so as to bring the intermitted tales together, he would have the effect again of a number of novelettes held together by a community of theme. It is especially noteworthy at this moment to observe that all but two of Prokosch's short stories which have appeared in periodicals are sections excerpted from his early novels. Apparently the editors who accepted them did not feel that they were unfinished. Nor are they. The novelette is a neglected but deeply satisfying form. A predilection for intensities, for language, and for the soul in a state of crisis is no advantage to the long novel; but to the shorter span of the story and novelette it is a great advantage. Lyricism and the novel are not good friends. Lyricism and the tale are inseparable companions.

In the words "tale" and "lyricism," we come to a final observation. Prokosch writes, "My earliest reading was (chiefly, or entirely in German) a vast number of fairy tales—Grimm and Anderson of course, and also French, Russian, Hindu. I can now see that these shaped my approach to narrative, even my style a little."[3] This self-analysis rings true. His ritualistic concept of character, his ritualistic concept of action, the imperative of movement from place to place, and, above all, the kaleidoscopic shudder in the rapid change of scene—these are all hallmarks of myth and fairy tale. Still, no modern writer ever truly writes pure fable. Like the rest of the moderns obsessed with myth—from Franz Kafka to Vladimir Nabokov—Prokosch tends to overlay myth with a coating of self-consciousness and of contemporary wit. In his work, one sees myth less as a wholehearted aim than as a sudden flash, like a trout breaking the surface of water, or a flake of mica revealed between the cleavage lines.

V *Envoi*

Wherever one turns in Prokosch's work he finds the oblique view, the irrational desire, the strange imbalance, the subtle mood, over all of which his style blows like a hectic wind in Hansel's and Gretel's forest. If one thinks Kafka took unpredictability as far as possible, he needs only to read Prokosch to know better. If one thinks T. S. Eliot's Apeneck Sweeney struck utter simplification in saying that life is "birth, copulation and death," one need only read Prokosch to find an author who strikes birth from the list. What, one asks, is the permanent worth of this novelist who stands outside the categories of the spokesmen for the mainstream, such as Thomas Mann, E. M. Forster, Ernest Hemingway, or William Faulkner? One ought to play it safe and say he honestly does not know. But that is too safe to be really safe.

It seems unlikely that more than two or three novels of Frederic Prokosch have any chance of survival. At the same time, it seems improbable that such a unique voice as his can ever be quite lost. No picture of the whole accomplishment of the twentieth century would be complete without cognizance of, say, *The Asiatics, The Seven Who Fled,* perhaps *Nine Days to Mukalla,* or *The Seven Sisters.* For these books possess the kind of delicate tensile strength, the individuality which survives longer than many a more conventional book. Not many people will read much of W. H. Hudson again, but no educated person will fail to read *Green Mansions.* And it is to the great eccentrics like Hudson or Huysmans or perhaps Frederick Rolfe (Baron Corvo) that one turns in order to "place" Frederic Prokosch. But this is to confess that one turns to *precedents* in literature, not to *traditions.* For such writers make their marks not by their influence on others but by the strength of their unyielding individuality. And while Prokosch's concern with the theme of a personal destiny linked with annihilation curiously prefigured some of the ideas of his friend Albert Camus, one could not say that Camus was influenced by Prokosch. And though Prokosch's poetry unquestionably affected the style of Dylan Thomas, the influence does not extend to others.

The modern scene does not offer equivalents to Frederic Prokosch. But even though he is not very much like any other contemporary novelist, his prospects are shared by other writers who, in rejecting the common view of life, are forced to create their own views through intensities of style and situation. They are, like Prokosch, essentially poets who in a century of prose, write novels. Julian Green, Lawrence Durrell, Vladimir Nabokov come to mind, along with Truman Capote, Carson McCullers, Paul Bowles, and possibly Isak Dinesen and James Purdy. In such a company, Frederic Prokosch has no masters—and hardly a peer.

Notes and References

Chapter One

1. "Contributors," *Story*, September-October, 1946, n.p.
2. The biographical material on Eduard Prokosch is blended from the following sources: Edwin H. Zaydel, "Eduard Prokosch, 1876-1938," *Modern Language Journal*, 23 (1938-39), 146; "Eduard Prokosch," New York *Times*, August 12, 1938, p. 17.
3. Other dates are given in some reference books. I have confirmed the date of May 17, 1906, with a certificate of birth.
4. "Contributors," *Story*, May, 1935, pp. 4, 9.
5. *Ibid.*
6. *Ibid.*
7. "Wimbledon," London *Spectator*, July 3, 1936, pp. 10-11.
8. Letter to R. Squires, December 8, 1962.
9. Richard C. Carpenter, "The Novels of Frederic Prokosch," *College English* (February, 1957), p. 262.
10. "Geoffrey Chaucer," *The English Novelists*, ed. Derek Verschoyle (London, 1936), pp. 4, 7, 9.
11. *Wilson Bulletin*, May, 1936, p. 570.
12. *New Statesman and Nation*, November 9, 1935, p. 699.
13. See dust jacket of *A Ballad of Love*.
14. *The Nation*, November 13, 1935, p. 572.
15. *Wilson Bulletin, loc. cit.*
16. See dust jacket of *Age of Thunder*.
17. London *Spectator*, June 26, 1936, p. 1184.
18. See dust jacket of *Age of Thunder*.
19. *Ibid.*
20. "Final Dreading," *The Collected Essays of John Peale Bishop* (New York and London, 1948), pp. 279-81.
21. "Books," New York *Herald Tribune*, August 29, 1937, p. 3.
22. *The Nation*, September 18, 1937, p. 296.
23. Fred B. Millett, *Contemporary American Authors* (New York, 1943), p. 533.
24. Boston *Evening Transcript*, October 28, 1939, p. 2.
25. *The New Yorker*, October 7, 1939, p. 76.
26. *New Statesman and Nation*, December 28, 1940, p. 687.
27. *The New Republic*, December 9, 1940, p. 800.
28. *The New Yorker*, December 28, 1940, p. 62.

29. Dayton Kohler, "Frederic Prokosch," *The English Journal,* (October, 1943), p. 419.

30. See "Isolationist America," London *Spectator,* May 10, 1940, p. 659.

31. See dust jacket of *The Skies of Europe.*

32. See *New Movies,* November 1944, p. 13.

33. *The New Republic,* November 13, 1944, p. 627.

34. *The New Yorker,* March 31, 1945, p. 81.

35. "Italy: Renascence from Rubble," *House and Garden,* June, 1948, pp. 112, 177.

36. New York *Times Book Review,* March 30, 1947, p. 12.

37. Harvey Breit, "In and Out of Books," New York *Times Book Review,* March 29, 1953, p. 8.

38. New York *Times Book Review,* March 22, 1953, p. 6.

39. *Saturday Review,* March 21, 1953, p. 15.

40. "Sea and Desert," *Commonweal,* May 1, 1953, p. 105.

41. See cover of Signet Edition of *The Asiatics.*

42. *Ibid.*

43. See dust jacket of *A Ballad of Love.*

44. See dust jacket of *The Seven Sisters.*

Chapter Two

1. Except where noted, citations of the poetry are made to *Chosen Poems* rather than to the volume in which the poem first appeared.

2. See Dylan Thomas, *Letters to Vernon Watkins,* ed. Vernon Watkins (London, 1957), pp. 29, 30, 32, 33, 35, 104.

3. "Biographical Note" facing title page of *Some Poems of Friedrich Hölderlin.*

Chapter Three

1. Letter to R. Squires, December 8, 1962.

2. *Atlantic Monthly,* November, 1945, p. 81.

Chapter Four

1. At the fateful picnic in *The Skies of Europe,* Philip pushes Saskia in a swing. She urges him to push her higher and higher. Barbezieux observes that the scene is "like a Fragonard" (374). In *A Ballad of Love,* though the dramatic situation is not identical, it is similar. The swinging episode is duplicated, and the identical comparison with

Fragonard's painting is made (187).

2. Letter to R. Squires, December 8, 1962.

3. *The Burning Cactus* (London, 1933), pp. 85-86.

4. "Yeats's Testament," *Poetry, A Magazine of Verse*, September, 1939, p. 338.

5. "Edith Sitwell," *A Celebration for Edith Sitwell*, ed. José Garcia Villa (New York, 1948), p. 35.

Chapter Five

1. See "Landscape—with Figures," *Vogue's First Reader*, Foreword by Frank Crowninshield (New York, 1942), pp. 110-16.

Chapter Six

1. Mark Schorer, Boston *Evening Transcript*, October 28, 1939, p. 2.

2. See dust jacket of *A Tale for Midnight*.

3. Citation of *The Seven Who Fled* is made for reasons of general availability to the second edition.

4. De la Scaze's name perhaps indicates the failure of his poetic attempts. *Scazon* is a classical meter and means "limping" or "halting."

5. This passage (272) is open to interpretation. Possibly it is intended to suggest that Barbara sees Alessandro with another lover. But on the basis of a later reference to obsessive photographs (340), I prefer to think it is these photographs that she sees.

6. The name "Cleophas" is not common, but Prokosch may have chosen it to bring to mind Le Sage's Don Cleofas in *Le Diable Boiteux* (1707). In Le Sage's satirical romance, Cleofas Zambulla with the help of a demon is able to reveal Parisian life. The name itself appears to be made up of two Greek roots and might be translated as "truthteller" or "tattletale." Certainly, Prokosch's Cleophas is an oblique means of revealing to the sisters their true natures.

Chapter Seven

1. "Credo of a Writer," *The Writer*, June, 1945, p. 167.

2. Letter to R. Squires, December 8, 1962.

3. *Ibid.*

Selected Bibliography

PRIMARY SOURCES

A. Novels

The Asiatics. New York and London: Harper and Brothers, 1935.
The Seven Who Fled. New York and London: Harper and Brothers, 1937.
Night of the Poor. New York and London: Harper and Brothers, 1939.
The Skies of Europe. New York and London: Harper and Brothers, 1941.
The Conspirators. New York and London: Harper and Brothers, 1943.
Age of Thunder. New York and London: Harper and Brothers, 1945.
The Idols of the Cave. Garden City, New York: Doubleday and Company, 1946.
Storm and Echo. Garden City, New York: Doubleday and Company, 1948.
Nine Days to Mukalla. New York: The Viking Press, 1953.
A Tale for Midnight. Boston: Little, Brown and Company, 1955.
A Ballad of Love. New York: Farrar, Straus and Cudahy, 1960.
The Seven Sisters. New York: Farrar, Straus and Cudahy, 1962.

B. Collections of Poetry

The Assassins. New York and London: Harper and Brothers, 1936.
The Carnival. New York and London: Harper and Brothers, 1938.
Death at Sea. New York and London: Harper and Brothers, 1940.
Chosen Poems. Garden City, New York: Doubleday and Company, 1948.

C. Translations

Some Poems of Friedrich Hölderlin. Norfolk, Connecticut: New Directions, 1943.
Love Sonnets by Louise Labé. New York: New Directions, 1947.
Medea. Greek Plays in Modern Translation, ed. Dudley Fitts, New York: The Dial Press, 1947.

D. Articles and Short Stories

"A Love Story." *Story,* VI (May, 1935), 18-25. A section of *The Asiatics.*
"Bandit." *Scribners Magazine,* XCVIII (September, 1935), 147-49. A section of *The Asiatics.*

"Geoffrey Chaucer." *The English Novelists.* Ed. Derek Verschoyle, London: Chatto and Windus, 1936.
"Russian Idyll." *Virginia Quarterly Review,* XIII (1937), 351-61. A section of *The Seven Who Fled.*
"Frederic Prokosch" (autobiographical letter). *Wilson Bulletin,* X (1935-36), 570.
"Yeats's Testament." *Poetry, a Magazine of Verse,* LIV (1939) 338-42.
"Isolationist America." London *Spectator,* CLXIV (1940), 659.
"Landscape—With Figures." *Vogue's First Reader.* Foreword, by Frank Crowninshield. New York: Julian Messner, 1942.
"Is Hollywood Dying?" *The New Republic,* CXI (1944), 627.
"Credo of a Writer." *The Writer,* LVIII (1945), 178.
"The Murderer." *Atlantic Monthly,* CLXXVI (1945), 78-82.
"The Flamingoes." *Story,* XXIX (1946), 67-72.
"Edith Sitwell." *A Celebration for Edith Sitwell,* ed. José Garcia Villa, New York: New Directions, 1948.
"Italy: Renascence from Rubble." *House and Garden* XCIII (1948), 112-13, 177.

SECONDARY SOURCES

BISHOP, JOHN PEALE. "Final Dreading." *The Collected Essays of John Peale Bishop.* New York and London: Charles Scribner's Sons, 1948. A review of *The Assassins* (originally published in *Poetry,* March 1937). Significant for Bishop's insights into Prokosch's relationship to Spengler and Perse.
CARPENTER, RICHARD C. "The Novels of Frederic Prokosch." College English XVIII (1957), 261-67. Illuminating account of the evolution of Prokosch's novels.
JONES, HOWARD MUMFORD. "Love and Geography." *Saturday Review,* XXXVI (March 21, 1953), 15. A review of *Nine Days to Mukalla.* Noteworthy for the critical comments on Prokosch's style.
KOHLER, DAYTON. "Frederic Prokosch." *The English Journal,* XXXII (1943), 413-19. Sympathetic criticism of Prokosch's early work.
MORSE, SAMUEL FRENCH. "Spectre Over Europe." *Poetry, a Magazine of Verse.* LIII (1938), 89-92. A review of *The Carnival.* An early criticism important both for its sympathies with and reservations toward the "romantic" aspects of Prokosch's poetry.

Index

Index

Ackerley, J. R., *Hindoo Holiday,* cited, 23
Allegory in *The Seven Who Fled,* 116-17
Analogy, use of, 142ff.
Anima in Prokosch, 141
Animals in imagery, 65, 100
Anti-intellectualism, 134ff.
Arnold, Matthew, 127
Artists in Prokosch novels, 75-81, 83-86
Auden, W. H., 41-42, 96

Bacon's *Novum Organum,* cited, 100
Bishop, John Peale, 26, 43; cited, 152
Bogan, Louise, 28
Bromfield, Louis, 26

Camus, Albert, 34, 147
Carpenter, Richard, error corrected, 26; cited, 152
Cenci, The, as theme, 33, 104-6
Chameleon as a symbol, 85
Character in the novels, 136-42
Characters, mythic nature of, 140, 145-46
Chaucer as influence, 21-22, 25
Childhood in Prokosch writings, 38
Classical symbolism suggested, 122-23
Cleophas as symbol, 122, 127, 150n
Comic character in Prokosch, 79
Commonweal, cited, 32
Communism, *see* Marxism
Connoly, Cyril, 23
Conspiracy as an instinct, 88

Corvo, Baron, 146
Creation in Prokosch, 78-79

Dapprich, Mathilde (mother), 17ff.
Deutsch, Babette, 31
Dolls as symbols, 105, 121; *see also* Puppetry
Durrell, Lawrence, 125

Eliot, T. S., 42; "Journey of the Magi," cited, 48; Apeneck Sweeney compared, 146
Euripides' *Medea,* translated by Prokosch, 31, 45-46
Evil, 102-6; definition, 115

Fadiman, Clifton, 27
Fairy tales, influence of, 145-46
Fascism, 79, 89, 133ff.
Faulkner, William, 46
Fitts, Dudley, 46
France, postwar, 31
Freedom, 95, 134ff.

Genet, Jean, 52
Geography, Prokosch influenced by, 24
Gide, André, 34, 114
Gorilla as symbol, 65
Gunther, John, 70

Hardy, Thomas, 46
Hawthorne's "Egotism, or the Bosom Serpent," cited, 63
Hemingway, Ernest, 70
Henreid, Paul, 29
Hero images, 128, 137ff.

History interpreted by Prokosch, 78-79
Hitler portrayed, 78
Hitlerism, 70, 77
Hölderlin, Friedrich, translated by Prokosch, 31, 45-46; influence on Prokosch, 37ff.
Homosexuality, 99, 105, 107-8, 122-23, 125
Horse as symbol, 73
Hudson, W. H., 146
Huysmans, Joris-Karl, 146

Illusion, utility of, 115
Innocence in Prokosch, 102-6
Intellectualism, 134ff.
Internationalism as theme, 131ff.
Isherwood, Christopher, 108
Islands as symbols, 126
Italy, postwar, 31

Jarrel, Randall, 27
Jeffers, Robinson, 26, 44
Jones, Howard Mumford, 32; cited, 152
Jung, Carl, 141

Kafka, Franz, compared, 146
Kazin, Alfred, 26
Koestler, Arthur, 90
Kohler, Dayton, cited, 152

Labé, Louise, translated by Prokosch, 31, 45-46
Lamarr, Hedy, 29
Le Sage, A. R., 150n
Lewis, Sinclair, 26
Life, Prokosch's view of, 112
Life symbols, 119
Limon, José, 80
Lisbon in wartime, 88

McCarthy, Mary, 26
MacLeish, Archibald, influence on Prokosch, 36ff.
Mann, Thomas, 34, 84
Marvell, Andrew, 63
Marxism, 133ff.

Maturity as a theme, 130
Maugham, Somerset, 34
Medieval literature, influence of, 22
Mercury, statue of, as symbol, 73-74
Meredith, George, 46
Metaphor, use of, 142ff.
Michelangelo's sonnets translated by Prokosch, 45
Millay, Edna St. Vincent, influence on Prokosch, 36ff.
Moore, Marianne, 34
Morse, Samuel French, cited, 152
Muir, Edwin, 26
Mythic nature of characters, 140, 145-46

Nationalism uncharacteristic of Prokosch, 138
Nature in Prokosch's writing, 38
Nazism, see Hitlerism
Negulesco, Jean, 29
New York in wartime, 96-98

Obsidian chip as symbol, 64-65
Old man's story as symbol, 73-74
Organization of the novels, 145-46
Orphan heroes, 128, 137

Pain, utility of, 115-16
Perse, St.-J., 152
Pornographic elements, 76, 103-4
Prokosch, Eduard (father), 17ff.
Prokosch, Frederic, ancestry, early years, education, and influences, 17ff.; athletics and sports, 20ff.; awards and prizes, 21, 25, 26, 33; as teacher, 22-25; friends, 25; return to America, 32; traveler, 21, 25, 26, 31, 33, 48-69 anthologized, 40, 46
evaluation of his work, 34-35, 146-47; Carpenter and Kohler cited, 152
poetry, 21, 27-28; analysis, 36-47
publishes Jeffers' poem, 26
reputation, decline of, 27, 30-31, 34

WRITINGS OF:

Articles and short stories, *see* "Selected Bibliography," 151-52
"The Chaucerian Apocrypha" (dissertation), 21-22
Unpublished novel, 22

Novels:

Age of Thunder, 30, 91-96
The Asiatics, 22-25, 48-53
A Ballad of Love, 19, 24, 33, 79-83
The Conspirators, 29, 87-91, 120
The Idols of the Cave, 30, 96-101
The Night of the Poor, 19, 27, 81, 102-6
Nine Days to Mukalla, 32, 61-69
The Seven Sisters, 33ff., 120-30
The Seven Who Fled, 26, 106-20
The Skies of Europe, 27-29, 70-79
Storm and Echo, 31ff., 54-61
A Tale for Midnight, 33, 102-6

Poetry—Collections:

The Assassins, 25ff., 36-41
The Carnival, 27, 41-44, 152
Chosen Poems, 31
Death at Sea, 27, 44-45

Poetry—particular poems:

"The Conspirators," 90; "The Dolls," 38-39; "The Fisherman," 37ff.; "Nocturne," 41; "Ode," 42-43; "Port Said," 39-40; "The Sand," 44-45; "Sunburned Ulysses," 44-45; "The Voyage," 36-37

Stories:

Bibliography, 151
"The Murderer," 68

Translations: 31, 45-46

Prokosch, Mathilde (mother), 17ff.
Puppetry, 20, 80; *see also* Dolls

Raine, Kathleen, 27, 44
Rimbaud, Arthur, paralleled in Prokosch, 83
Roberts, Michael, 26
Rolfe, Frederick, 146

Saint-Exupéry, Antoine de, dedication to, 91
Saint-Léger, Alexis, *Anabase,* cited, 48-49; *see also* Perse, St.-J., 152
Santayana, George, dedication to, 61
Scharper, Philip J., 32
Schorer, Mark, 27, 103
Sexuality, 120ff.
Shawn, Ted, 80
Shelley's *The Cenci,* cited, 104ff.
Sins, seven deadly, 115
Sitwell, Edith, 86
Snakes as symbols, 121
Spender, Stephen, 84
Spengler, Oswald, 132, 152
Spenser, *The Faerie Queene,* cited, 63
Structure of the novels, 145-46
Style of the novels, 7, 142-45
Symbolism, 119
Symbols in Prokosch: analogy, use of, 142ff.; animals, 100; *Cenci, The,* 33, 104-6; chameleon, 85; classical, 122-23; Cleophas, 122, 127, 150n; dolls, 105, 121; fairy tales, influence of, 145-46; gorilla, 65; horse, toy, 73; heroes, 128, 137; islands, 126; life symbols, 119; Mercury, statue of, 73-74; metaphor, use of, 142ff.; mythic nature of characters, 140, 145-46; obsidian chip, 64-65; old man's story, 73-74; snakes, 121; zoo imagery, 100

Theme in the novels, 130, 131-36
Thomas, Dylan, influenced by Prokosch, 40-41, 147

Venice, postwar, 31
Vidal, Gore, 32

War, peripheries of, in novels, 87-101
Watkins, Vernon, 40
Whitman, Walt, 102
Wilder, Thornton, 26, 34
Williams, Oscar, 40
Wilson, Edmund, 30

Wordsworth, William, 37
World War II, effect on Prokosch novels, 7, 87-101

Yeats, William Butler, influence on Prokosch, 25ff., 37ff., 118-19; *Last Poems and Two Plays,* cited, 86

Zoo in imagery, 100